Middle Eastern Cookery

Middle Eastern Cookery

ROBIN HOWE

Illustrated by Tony Streek

Eyre Methuen London

First published 1978
by Eyre Methuen Ltd
11 New Fetter Lane, London EC4P 4EE

ISBN 0 413 38220 6

Printed in Great Britain by
Hazell Watson & Viney Ltd
Aylesbury, Bucks

Contents

Introduction

Probably no other region on earth has suffered as many invasions as the area which we today call the Middle East and which over the centuries has been the battlefield of mighty empires, including the Persian, Byzantine and Islamic and, in more recent times, the Ottoman. The invaders came and went but usually remained long enough to stage lavish banquets which have become legendary, for descriptions of these fabulous meals have been passed down through the ages in songs and poems. And every invader, we are told, left behind a record of his national dishes, thus giving credit to the claim that the region has one of the biggest collections of recipes in the world. Such was the interest in food that manuals were compiled giving careful instructions on its cooking and serving, also of its health-giving properties. Thus was created a history of food which has become as much an integral part of the region's history as its wars and conquests.

The ebb and flow of military hosts with the inevitable intermingling of populations and absorption of living habits, particularly in the cooking field, leave us today with the impossible task of tracing the dishes of the Middle East. The Greeks lay claim to much of what we call Turkish cooking; the Iranians plead similarly, while the Iraqis, whose Caliphs in the great days of the Baghdad Courts, are said to have possessed a cooking repertoire that could sustain a new dish for every day of the year. This does not mean that there are no recipes indigenous to any one country, although claims for a particular recipe as being definitely local cannot always be proved. Throughout the region, from Greece through to Iran, there is a closely knit pattern of cooking with only here and there a local adaptation. There are those who feel, not always willingly, that most of today's regional dishes are of Turkish origin. Some doubtless are, but this belief stems from the development of fine cooking in the kitchens of the erstwhile royal palaces. However, it cannot be denied that the Turks have exerted an enormous influence on the development of regional cooking, not only in the Middle East but also in the Balkans. As a people they are proud of their long tradition of fine cooking, summed up perhaps by an old Turkish saying: 'A hungry bear won't dance'.

Despite the traditional nature of cooking in the Middle East, the wind of change is blowing. Even here servants are less easy to come by, and kitchens are now filled with modern gadgets, since fewer and fewer people are anxious to pound and knead the live-long day as they once appeared to be doing. With the adoption of modern gadgets, in some areas there has been a graceful acceptance of Western dishes – particularly, but not surprisingly, from France.

One might imagine that the cooking of the Israelis would be quite different from that of the area in general. It was once described to me as 'like a monster cooking pot simmering with different flavours, different combinations, with dishes coming from all over the world'. Ironically, the Arab influence on Israeli dishes is strong and quite a number of recipes given in this book as being of Arab origin, or even Turkish, are claimed equally as Israeli.

Here it is worth noting a remark made by a friend, a diplomat living in Israel, at the time when she heard I was compiling this book: 'What a wonderful idea this is, to bring together all those disputatious brothers of the Middle East.' This is what I hope in some small measure this book will achieve.

Finally, an ancient Persian chronicler wrote that the true happiness for the gourmet is when he has actually chosen what he will eat. And, to adapt an old Persian saying: 'You cannot appreciate the flavour of the halva unless you try it', I hope that the following recipes will let you 'taste the halva' and appreciate the flavour of Middle Eastern food.

Acknowledgements

Together with my ex-journalist husband, a trencherman, I spent a considerable time in the Middle East. I must acknowledge his willing assistance, albeit not entirely altruistic. Also, on a more practical level, I would like to thank my friends and their cooks in the region, in particular my own cook in Beirut, and the cook of an old friend in Cairo who, in fact, gave me my first unforgettable taste of Arab food. In Istanbul I had two cooks – not at the same time – curiously both Turkish born but of Greek extraction, so that our cooking was Turco-Greek. And so it goes on throughout the East Mediterranean. Apart from cooks, I am greatly indebted to the Turkish Government, in particular Nejat M. Sönmez, then of the Turkish Embassy in London, and Altemur Kiliç, then of Ankara.

In compiling this book I have written to many old friends to check and cross-check recipes but none, out of modesty, will let me acknowledge their help. The reply of one was typical of them all: 'Everyone knows I cannot cook, and all my recipes come from my cook.' However, I would like to mention two Israelis, neither of whom have I met but who gave me much assistance, Mrs Tamar Yuval of Jerusalem, and Mr Jack Barnett, Director of Israel Information in London.

Porto Maurizio

Measurements

It is not always easy or with absolute accuracy to convert metric into Imperial measures, or cups into ounces, etc, to say nothing of such measurements as *okes*, *drams*, *rotls*, *hoogias*, and the 'size of a pigeon's egg'. Fortunately, absolute accuracy in the kitchen is seldom required; with cakes and pastries yes, or even for beginners, although with time one learns that a little bit extra or less here and there with stews, sauces, soups, etc. is not important – it might even be an improvement. Working on Arab recipes for some cooks could be exasperating, for timing and accuracy in the kitchen is not a characteristic among the Arabs or, for that matter, among the rest of the people of the Middle East. As one Lebanese friend told me: 'If we keep a dish on the stove for 10 minutes longer, or if some ingredient is not in the kitchen, or we forget it, what does it matter?' I have a Bagdadi cookbook which tells me that '16 tablespoons equal a round 50 cigarette tin', but does not state whether for a British or American spoon, and here there is a difference. But it all sorts itself out in the end.

Therefore, when studying these recipes, remember that everything is approximate. If a recipe simply says '2 cups' without adding the US equivalent, this means that cups from either side of the Atlantic will do. If 2–3 spoons, then it means just what it says, and spoons of either British or American size can be used.

As far as serving portions are concerned, here there is even more disparity. People in the Middle East do not usually cook for a set number; they cook to allow for unexpected guests.

By traditional standards of hospitality, even casual droppers-in are asked to stay and eat. In Iraq, if asked to eat with a local family, you may always bring another guest along with you without embarrassment or even without forewarning your hostess. Such guests are known as your 'slipper' (*qabqah*) and receive the same welcome as you. Therefore, view the serving portions in this book as a guideline, for, apart from 'stretching' for guests, some people eat like dwarfs, others like giants.

Throughout this book metric, British and American measurements have been used and, wherever possible, ingredients have been measured in cups and tablespoons for easy conversion. The metric measurement has been printed first, followed by the British and American equivalents in brackets. All spoon measurements are level throughout this book unless otherwise stated. The cups and spoons used for British and American measurements are standard. Approximate conversions are as follows:

2¼lb	1kg
1½lb	675g
1lb	450g
¾lb	340g
½lb	225g
¼lb	110g
1oz	30g

1l	1¾pt	4⅜ cups US
¾l	1¼pt	3⅛ cups US
560ml	1pt	2½ cups US
420ml	¾pt	1⅞ cups US
280ml	½pt	1¼ cups US
140ml	¼pt	⅝ cup US

Glossary

Dried Beans. These are a feature of Middle Eastern cooking and sometimes it is difficult to say for how long they should cook. Fresh stocks of beans often need very little soaking, although all local recipes from this region suggest doing this overnight and even longer. Too long soaking will possibly cause fermentation. As far as actual cooking time is concerned, this again varies with the freshness and quality of the beans. I have had some which have taken up to three hours, and some which have cooked in under the hour. Dried beans can be cooked in a pressure cooker, but it is important that the cooker is never more than half-filled with water and beans, in fact, it is safer to restrict to one-third full.

Clarified Butter. Popular as a cooking medium in many parts of the Middle East, especially the Lebanon. Butter is melted in a pan and about one-third of its volume in water is added. It is then boiled for a short time and strained into a jar. When it is quite cold, the layer of pure fat which rests on the top is carefully taken off, leaving the water and impurities behind.

Chick-peas. Chick-peas are hard, round and corn-coloured; somewhat earthy in flavour. Most varieties require long soaking and about one hour cooking. They are extensively cultivated in the Middle East as they are considered nourishing.

Coriander. A lacy-leafed herb whose seeds and leaves are widely used in Mediterranean cooking. Its leaves are used as one uses parsley; the seeds are usually crushed.

Croûtons. Sippets of bread fried and served as a garnish. Cut a slice of stale bread as for toast, remove the crusts and cut the rest into dice, not too small or, when fried, they will be like small shot. Heat a little fat until smoking-hot and quickly fry the diced bread, stirring all the time. Drain before serving.

Cubeb. The berry of a climbing plant, a native of Java. It resembles pepper and has a pungent spicy flavour, much appreciated in eastern cooking.

Cumin Seeds. Aromatic seeds with a slightly bitter flavour obtained from a small annual herb which belongs to the parsley family. They are native to the Mediterranean and resemble caraway seeds in appearance and flavour. Used both in sweet and savoury dishes.

Fat in Cooking. In the Lebanon and neighbouring countries, *samnah*, clarified butter (qv) is used; the Turks prefer butter usually, while other countries use vegetable shortening. See also **Oils**.

Fenugreek. Both the leaves and the seeds of this plant are used in cooking. It is a native of West Asia but gets its name from the Latin *Fenugraecum*, which means Greek hay. The plant, rather like a tall clover, is grown as a crop. Its flavour resembles celery; the seeds are sand-coloured and they come in varying sizes.

Flour. Plain flour (all-purpose) should be used unless otherwise called for in the following recipes.

Lentils. These are widely used in the Middle East and are the seeds of a small plant with pods and are sold in their dry state. Lentils may be cooked without previous soaking but if you want them to keep their shape it is better to soak them at least one hour before cooking; they will also cook more quickly. If using lentils as a purée, pre-soaking is not needed.

Marjoram. A herb native to the Mediterranean. Its flavour is spicy, sweet, scented and akin to thyme which it often replaces in some dishes. It can be used in a variety of dishes, with vegetables, meat dishes, omelettes, etc. See **Oregano**.

Numi Basrah. Dried limes used to give flavour to savoury dishes and pilaus in Iraq and Iran.

Oils. Undoubtedly olive oil is the most popular oil for cooking in the Middle East, although other oils are used as well. The Jews favour corn or nut oil, the Copts sesame. For deep frying of fish, olive oil is usually preferred and, throughout the region, olive oil is always used for dishes to be served cold for it does not congeal. Olive oil varies considerably and most of the oil of this region is inclined to be strongly flavoured and somewhat heavy. However, it is the oil of the area and a blander oil does not quite give the same authentic flavour.

Olives. There are countless varieties of olives, and size has nothing to do with their flavour, which is influenced by their locality, the soil and the altitude in which they are grown. Olives are not merely something to nibble with drinks, in the countries where they prosper they are used extensively in cooking and also in salads.

Oregano. The name by which wild marjoram is commonly known. It is a difficult herb to describe since its species are numerous. One of its problems is the fact that plants of the same species, when grown in different climates and soils, produce quite different flavours. The best that can be said in general, is the flavour of oregano is stronger than sweet marjoram, and is pleasant and aromatic. See **Marjoram**.

Parsley. This well-known herb probably comes originally from the Middle East. There are several varieties but the plain leafed parsley, rather like chervil but with a much stronger flavour, is more generally used in the cooking of the region.

Pastry. *Phyllo* (Greek) and *Yufka* (Turkish) pastry is a plain, paper-thin pastry used in Greece and Turkey in particular and more or less throughout the Middle East, to make savoury and sweet dishes. It can be made at home but it does require the hand of the expert. It can be bought in many continental stores, especially those owned by Greeks and Cypriots. One pound of pastry will give about 24, or perhaps a few more, sheets.

Pine-nuts. The elongated white kernels of pine cones used extensively in Middle Eastern cooking. They remain fresh for a considerable time. Sadly they are expensive everywhere. In this book I have kept the original quantities called for but these can be halved or quartered as price dictates.

Pistachios. The nuts of a small deciduous tree, a species of the turpentine tree, which has a green kernel used in various ways. They can be roasted and salted, grated and sprinkled over milk puddings, or used as a flavouring and colouring for ice-cream.

Pomegranate. A very common fruit in Iran where, in addition to being eaten raw, it is also used in stews, soups and sauces. It is probably a native of Iran, and was mentioned in the *Old Testament*, but was certainly known to the ancient Greeks and the Hindus. The outer, thin and somewhat leathery skin of the pomegranate varies from pale yellow to mauve in colour, but the flesh inside is a bright red. In good quality fruit the seeds within are tender, juicy and easy to eat.

Quince. Although one of the earliest of cultivated garden fruits – we are told it was with a quince that the devil lured Eve from the path of righteousness – today in the West it is one of the least cultivated. In ancient times quinces offered at a marriage feast assured love and happiness. Maybe we should return the quince to our gardens. Although the Western housewife considers quinces are only for jams and conserves, the Iranian housewife is more adventurous, stuffing them with as much enthusiasm as she does peppers and tomatoes. Raw quinces have a tart, somewhat astringent flavour; cooked they are sweet and delicious. There are several varieties of the fruit, which grow on small trees, the most usual being a pale golden colour, pear- or apple-shaped.

Rocket. A herb with an interesting and pungent flavour, much used in the Mediterranean as a salad herb, usually combined with sweeter herbs, and served with a dressing of oil and vinegar.

Saffron. This comes from the orange-coloured stigmas of a mauve crocus. It is an expensive spice because the stigmas have to be picked by hand and over 200,000 are required to make a pound of saffron. Only a small amount is required in cooking, but this gives an aroma and a yellowish colour to many dishes. It is widely used in Iranian cooking.

Sesame Seeds. Sesame is an aromatic annual herb. Its seeds vary in colour and when toasted have the flavour of toasted almonds. Used considerably in Middle Eastern cooking and can be bought whole or ground.

Spices. Every country, one might almost say almost every cook, has its own preferred combination of spices and herbs. For example, a favourite Lebanese spice mixture consists of one part cayenne pepper, two of sweet paprika pepper, and two parts of ground cinnamon. Another popular Arab combination locally called *talkia*, is ground coriander seeds fried together with crushed garlic, which is reminiscent of Indian mixtures. Today almost all spices of the world can be bought in the supermarkets as well as the Greek and Indian shops and there should be no difficulty obtaining any of the spices required for the recipes in this book.

Sumac. Known generally as a decorative plant which produces seeds, some varieties of which are ground to a red-purple powder, or used whole, in which case they are coarsely crushed, soaked in water for 20 minutes or so, then squeezed thoroughly to extract the juice. The flavour of *sumac* is lightly astringent, and rather sour. The Romans used it before the arrival of lemons. It is used throughout the Middle East, especially in the Lebanon.

Tahina. This is a rather thin paste made from sesame seeds crushed in a mill. The great Middle East favourite, it is combined with other ingredients to make a local form of salad, or dip, and served with Arab bread.

Turmeric. Sometimes called 'the poor man's saffron' for, if used in minute quantities, it will give to a dish almost the same colour as saffron, i.e. yellow. It is the fleshy root of a plant, a member of the ginger family.

Its aroma is clean, but its flavour, such as it is, is rather bitter and faintly resinous.

Yogurt. Yoghurt in Turkey; Yaourti in Greece, Laban in Syria, Iraq and Lebanon, and Leban in Egypt. This cultured milk is essential to the Middle Eastern kitchen as its acidity is considered a diet regulator. Legend has it that the secret of souring milk was whispered in the ear of Patriarch Abraham by an angel. Cultures made by a starter, *Lactobacillus acidophilus*, are kept going in Middle Eastern kitchens all the time.

Yogurt varies from a smooth creamy curd, light in texture and aroma, to one which is heavy, with an almost beery odour, thick and full of bubbles. Locally, sheep milk is preferred in its preparation, but excellent yogurt also is made with goat, camel and buffalo milk. Cows' milk yogurt has less flavour but is considered more digestible.

Yogurt is used in cooking, with meat, vegetables or fruit. Sheep or goat milk yogurt does not curdle with cooking, but the lighter yogurts, such as we are used to in the West, often do. So they require to be stabilized to prevent this (see below).

Yogurt can be used as a sauce, a cheese, in puddings, and is an important ingredient in many salad dressings. In Iraq it is eaten chilled with fresh dates, or with date syrup, or sugar, as a summer breakfast dish, although in Turkey it is considered exceedingly odd to eat yogurt at breakfast time. For the Turks, it is something to eat between meals, indeed, the cult of yogurt amongst the Turks is ancient. Turkish yogurt is almost butter-thick and usually sold in round cans or earthenware bowls. It is not unusual for families to make an excursion to a favourite yogurt dealer to eat a bowl of his product under the shade of a plane tree, and carry back bowls of it for home consumption. Indeed, there are eating houses selling almost exclusively yogurt to which the people flock. In most towns the yogurt man calls daily with his twin tubs of fresh yogurt swinging from chains suspended from a yoke across his shoulders.

In Arab countries it is customary to place a bowl of yogurt

on the table to be eaten with such varied foods as omelettes, stuffed vegetables, stews, salads and kebabs. It is often flavoured with salt, dried and almost powdered mint, or garlic.

Never keep yogurt too long, even in a refrigerator, otherwise it will turn sour. To stabilize yogurt, take 2½ cups (3 US) yogurt, 1 egg white, 1 tablespoon (1¼ US) cornflour, and salt to taste. Pour the yogurt into a pan and put on a low heat. Lightly beat the egg white. Mix the cornflour with enough water to make a thin paste. Stir this into the yogurt and when it thickens add the egg white, stirring all the time in one direction only. Add salt and bring slowly to the boil: reduce the heat to minimum and cook uncovered for about 10 minutes, or until it is thick. It is now ready for cooking without any fear of curdling.

Starters and Salads

If food is a matter for serious thought in the Middle East, then the *mezé* (starters) are a way of life into which much of the culinary wisdom of the area has gone. No one is quite sure of their origin, although discussions are weighty and solemn with each country laying claim to their invention, except perhaps Iraq and Iran where the cult of the starter is not so developed. However, the origin of the name is not in dispute, for it is claimed the word *mezza* came via the Genovese traders in this region centuries ago. And the name? In Greece they are called *mezethakia*; in Turkey *mezéler*, usually shortened to *mezé*, and in Arab countries they are *al mezah*, or *maza* and *mezze*.

In the main, starters are served with *rakı* (see page 183) or wine but also with coffee, scalding hot tea, with beer and even some of the more syrupy soft drinks. They vary from the few simple offerings of villagers to the fifty or more dishes served in elegant restaurants. But wherever served, they are designed to 'open' the appetite, to be savoured with feelings of peace, with conversation and never hurried.

Apart from the starters for which recipes have been given in this chapter, there is usually a colourful assortment of staples which are brought before any drink is served. Among the many cold items one finds olives of all kinds, tomatoes usually cut into chunks, strips of ice-cold cucumber, salted nuts and, when in season, fresh almonds, walnuts or hazelnuts (incidentally, no self-respecting Arab or Turk would set out on a journey without a pocketful of nuts), salty goat or sheep cheese, slices of pastirma flavoured with garlic and paprika, a type of beef-bacon, various kinds of sausages, some well garlicked, others stuffed with pistachio nuts; even fruits make an appearance, apples, oranges, cherries, peppered figs, pickled lemons, green and somewhat bitter. In the Lebanon they serve not only raw *kibbeh* (see page 148) but also raw liver, taken from the calf killed the same morning. Also very popular in Turkey and Greece are rice-stuffed mussels, and throughout the region vine leaf *dolmas* are a must. 'Once upon a time' one was also served black and red caviar, also *taramasalata* but, alas, only in the really elegant spots these days, and at a price.

Among the hot dishes we find sizzling hot, minute meat balls, grilled or fried liver or kidneys, small fried fish and swordfish kebabs. In the Arab world *kibbeh* in all its guises appears, and throughout the area tiny, hot *börekler* or pasties, as well as fried brains and mussels dipped in batter and fried in oil. One could go on endlessly, the choice stops only with the imagination of the cook.

In the recipes in this chapter it is not always possible to stipulate the exact number of portions the dish will make, for many are dips or salads and these are expandable since one usually scoops up small portions of each to go with other items, or simply to taste.

My Lady's Salad

HANIM SALATA (Syria)

heart of small white cabbage, shredded
2–3 stalks celery, finely chopped
6 spring onions, sliced
salt and pepper
1 tablespoon (1¼ US) mild vinegar
450g (1lb) boiled chicken, shredded
3–4 hard-boiled eggs, quartered
1 cup (1¼ US) dressing (see page 71)
about 12 black olives, stoned

Combine the cabbage, celery, onions, salt and pepper with the vinegar and arrange in a salad bowl. Cover with the chicken and eggs. Add the dressing, garnish with the olives and chill.

Aubergine Purée or 'Poor Man's Caviar'

PATLICAN SALATASI (Turkey)

This dish is eaten throughout the Middle East, the name varying in each country, the recipe but slightly.

2–3 aubergines
1 medium-sized onion, minced
1 tablespoon (1¼ US) finely chopped parsley
3 tablespoons (3¾ US) olive oil
salt and black pepper
juice 1 small lemon

Grill or bake the aubergines whole until the skins are black and blistered. Cool, peel and mash the flesh. Pound to a purée in a mortar, or purée in a blender together with the onion. (If pounding, add the onion when the aubergine is soft.) When the aubergine is puréed, gradually add the olive oil until the mixture is of a thick mayonnaise consistency. Pour into a bowl, sprinkle with parsley, salt, pepper and lemon juice and serve chilled.

The nicest way to eat this kind of purée is with brown bread, using it as a scoop.

In Iraq crushed sesame seeds, dried mint and pomegranate seeds are added to the basic recipe, also crushed garlic. In Iran, vinegar as well as lemon juice is added, plus garlic and ground cinnamon. The Jordanians mix the aubergine with mayonnaise instead of olive oil and often add diced cucumber and tomatoes.

Fried Aubergine with Yogurt

PATLICAN YOǦURTLU (Turkey)

For 4–6

2–3 long aubergines
salt
olive oil for frying
2–3 cloves (or more) garlic, crushed
2 cups (2½ US) yogurt

Slice the aubergines without peeling into thick rounds. Sprinkle with salt and leave between two plates for 30 minutes with a weight on top to draw out their bitter liquid. Rinse in running water, pat dry and fry in hot oil until brown. Drain, place on a warm dish and keep hot. Mix the garlic with the yogurt and pour this over the aubergines. Serve at once.

Aubergine Dip or Aubergine with Sesame Oil Sauce

BABA GHANNOUGE or BATINJAAN BI TAHEENI (Middle East)

The Lebanese call this dish *la Coquette*, the recipe for which, it is claimed, goes back to the days of the Sultans when one of the beauties of the Royal Harem reputedly invented the recipe to gain the Sultan's favour.

4–6 cloves garlic
salt to taste
2–3 large aubergines
1 cup ($1\frac{1}{4}$ US) tahina (see page 20)
juice 1 lemon
mint or parsley, chopped
pomegranate seeds (optional)
olive oil

Crush and pound the garlic with salt. Grill the aubergines over an open flame until the skins blister and crack open, or bake them in a hot oven. Pull off the skins, chop up the flesh, then pound or blend the flesh until it is a purée. Alternately beat in the lemon juice and *tahina* until a smooth sauce is obtained. (If putting the aubergine flesh through an electric blender, do so in small quantities. Beat the flesh first and mix in some of the lemon juice and *tahina* before blending.) Pour the sauce into a bowl and garnish with mint or parsley and pomegranate seeds. Serve cold. Just before serving, a little olive oil may be dribbled over the top. Serve with Arab or soft dark bread.

Green Bean Salad

SALATIT EL LOUBDIEH (Middle East)

225g ($\frac{1}{2}$lb) cold cooked French beans
2 tablespoons ($2\frac{1}{2}$ US) olive oil
1 tablespoon ($1\frac{1}{4}$ US) lemon juice
garlic to taste, crushed

Break the beans into pieces. Mix the oil, lemon and garlic and pour over the top.

Carrot and Orange Salad

SALAT GEZER-HAI (Israel)

For 4–6

225g (½lb) firm young carrots
juice 3 oranges and ½ lemon
salt and pepper
pinch ground ginger (optional)

Wash, scrape and coarsely grate the carrots. Put into a small salad bowl, cover with orange and lemon juice, add salt and pepper to taste, ginger, if using, and leave in the refrigerator 24 to 36 hours to let the carrots absorb the flavours. Serve with lettuce or garnished with fresh mint leaves.

Grapefruit and Potato Salad

SALAT ESHCOLIOT VE'TAPUHEI ADAMA (Israel)

For 4–6

2 medium-sized grapefruit
½kg (about 1 lb) cold boiled potatoes
1 small mild onion, thinly sliced
1 small red or green pepper

Dressing
salt and pepper
1 tablespoon (1¼ US) vinegar
2 tablespoons (2½ US) olive oil

Peel the grapefruit and divide into segments, pulling off all pith and skin. Put into a salad bowl. Dice the potatoes and place on top of the grapefruit, add the onion. Discard the core and seeds of the pepper, finely chop the flesh and sprinkle it over the top of the salad.

To make the dressing, mix the ingredients in the order given and whisk until frothy, or put into a bottle and shake well. Dry mustard can be added if liked.

Add the dressing to the salad and chill before serving.

Mushroom Salad

BORANI GARCH (Iran)

For 4–6

½kg (about 1lb) fresh mushrooms
2–3 tablespoons olive oil
1 large onion, finely chopped
salt and pepper
½–¾ cup yogurt
dried mint, crushed

Wash, pat dry and thickly slice the mushrooms. Heat the oil, add the onion and when it begins to change colour add the mushrooms. Cook for 5 minutes. Take from the pan and leave until cool. Add salt and pepper, cover with yogurt and gently mix. Chill and just before serving sprinkle with dried mint.

Orange, Onion and Olive Salad

MUNKACZINA (Middle East)

For 4–6

1–2 large oranges or lemons
1–2 large onions, thinly sliced
black olives, stoned
salt and red pepper
1 tablespoon (1¼ US) olive oil

Thinly slice the oranges or lemons. Cut off the peel and remove the pips. Arrange the slices at the bottom of a shallow dish. Spread the onions over the top. Garnish with olives, sprinkle with salt, red pepper and oil.

Peppers in Yogurt

BIBER YOĞURTLU (Turkey)

For 4–6

2–3 medium-sized sweet peppers
2 tablespoons (2½ US) olive oil
1 cup (1¼ US) yogurt
salt and olive oil

Slice off the tops of the peppers, remove the cores and seeds and cut the flesh into long strips. Heat the oil and sauté the strips of pepper until soft. Cut into smaller pieces and put into a bowl. Pour the yogurt over the top, stir gently, sprinkle lightly with salt and add a *few* drops of olive oil.

Tomato Salad

DOMATES SALATASI (Turkey)

For 4–6

4 large tomatoes
1 medium-sized onion
2 green peppers
salt
1–1½ tablespoons olive oil
3–4 tablespoons vinegar
black olives, stoned

Thinly slice the tomatoes and onion. Remove the stems, cores and seeds from the peppers and cut the flesh into strips. Combine these ingredients and sprinkle with salt. Mix the oil and vinegar, pour this over the salad and garnish with black olives.

Turnips Cooked with Beetroots

MAYI (Iraq)

A popular winter dish of steaming hot 'pink' turnips sold from barrows in the main streets of Iraqi towns. '*Mayi, mayi*' the vendors cry, and you can buy a plate of hot turnips at any time of the day, for *mayi* is considered as something to be eaten between meals.

Mayi is simple to prepare. Wash, peel and slice as many turnips as required and cook them with half their quantity of cooked, sliced beetroots in plenty of unsalted water until soft. Drain, sprinkle lightly with salt – the dish should preserve its sweet beetroot flavour – and serve hot. Do not discard the water, the Iraqis say it is good to drink as an aid to digestion.

Yogurt with Cucumber

MAST VA KHIAR (Iran)

For 4–6

1 large cucumber
2 cups (2½ US) yogurt
salt and pepper
1 tablespoon (1¼ US) chopped fresh dill, or 1 teaspoon (1¼ US) dry dill

Peel the cucumber and cut into dice; combine with the yogurt, add the herbs and seasonings, mix well and chill.

Egyptian Bean Salad

FOUL MADUMNAS (Egypt)

For 6

1kg (2¼lb) dried beans, white or brown
2–4 cloves garlic
olive oil
lemons
hard-boiled eggs
salt and pepper

Soak the beans overnight in water, drain and cook in fresh unsalted water until tender but not mushy. Drain and place in a bowl. Serve separately crushed or finely chopped garlic, a jug of olive oil, quartered lemons, hard-boiled eggs (preferably Beid Hamine eggs (see page 50), salt and pepper. It is usual to break up an egg with a fork and mix into the beans, adding condiments, garlic, oil and lemon to taste.

Instead of dried beans, good quality canned beans may be used.

Haricot Bean Salad

KURU FASULYA PIYAZI (Turkey and Middle East)

For 4–6

225g ($\frac{1}{2}$lb) dried haricot beans
onion, thinly sliced
parsley, chopped
red or green pepper, chopped
hard-boiled egg, chopped
tomato, chopped
black olives, stoned and chopped
vinegar or lemon juice
olive oil

Soak the beans for 24 hours, drain and cook them in fresh unsalted water until tender. Leave in their liquid until cold. Drain well and place in a shallow dish. Cover with the sliced and chopped ingredients, all to taste, and sprinkle with vinegar or lemon juice. Finally pour olive oil over the lot.

Canned haricot beans may be used in the same way.

Chick-Pea Salad

SALATIT HUMMUS MASLOUQ or HUMMUS BI TAHINA (Middle East)

For 4–6

For this 'salad' you can use either dried or canned chick-peas. Dried chick-peas require long soaking, 18 to 20 hours. Cook until very soft in unsalted water for at least one hour. Cooking time depends on the age and freshness of the chick-peas; in a pressure cooker they will take about 20 minutes. Whether the chick-peas come from a can or the pan, they must be thoroughly drained.

225g (½lb) chick-peas, or 2 cans net weight 400g (14oz) each
½ cup (⅔ US) lemon juice
½ cup (⅔ US) tahina (see page 20)
2 cloves garlic, crushed
salt to taste

Garnish
olive oil
parsley, chopped
pomegranate seeds (optional)
sumac (see page 20) *or paprika pepper*

Put aside about 12 chick-peas for use as a garnish. Put the rest through the finest blade of a mincer, or blend to a purée. If using a mincer, mash the chick-peas after mincing, then add the remaining ingredients in the order given (not the garnish) and beat to a purée. If blending, put just a little water and the lemon juice at the bottom of the goblet, add the chick-peas, *tahina*, and salt and blend to a thick purée. Turn the purée into a shallow bowl, swirl it round to form a well in the centre into which dribble a little oil and garnish with the whole chick-peas, parsley, pomegranate seeds and *sumac*.

Although listed as a 'salad' this is more of a dip, served in the Middle East with Arab bread used as a scoop.

Broad Bean Croquettes

FALAFIL or TĀĀMIA (Egypt)

These have been described as Mediterranean 'hot dogs' and are credited as the national dish of both Egypt and Israel, although the Christian Copts claim them exclusively as their own invention. During Lenten and other feasts, when the Copts are not allowed to eat meat, they prepare *falafil* in large quantities. There are several spellings and recipes for them; my recipe comes from a Copt friend from Upper Egypt.

1kg ($2\frac{1}{4}$lb) broad beans
$\frac{1}{4}$–$\frac{1}{2}$ head garlic, chopped
2 medium-sized onions, chopped
small quantity of parsley and dill, chopped
salt, cayenne pepper and coriander seeds to taste
pinch bicarbonate of soda
sesame seeds
oil for deep frying

Soak the beans overnight in cold water. Drain well. Mix the garlic, onions, herbs and beans and grind twice through the finest blade of a mincer. Add seasonings, coriander seeds and bicarbonate of soda and leave for 15 minutes. Cut the mixture into small rounds, shape into balls roughly the size of a walnut. With slightly wet hands, press a few sesame seeds on the top of each ball. Heat the fat to smoking-hot and, using a frying basket, fry the balls until a dark golden brown. Drain on absorbent paper and serve hot.

Both in Egypt and Israel there are *falafil* stands at almost every street corner in the large towns.

Egg Salad

YUMURTA SALATASI (Turkey)

For 4

3–4 hard-boiled eggs, sliced
1 medium-sized onion, finely sliced
2 tablespoons ($2\frac{1}{2}$ US) lemon juice
1 tablespoon ($1\frac{1}{4}$ US) olive oil
$\frac{1}{4}$–$\frac{1}{2}$ teaspoon sugar
finely chopped parsley to taste
salt and pepper

Arrange the eggs on a flat dish and spread the onion over the eggs. Mix the oil and lemon juice, beat well, add the remaining ingredients and pour this dressing over the top.

Fried Brains

BEYIN TAVASI (Turkey)

For 6

3 sets sheep brains
4 cups (5 US) water
1 tablespoon ($1\frac{1}{4}$ US) vinegar
1 small onion, quartered
seasoned flour
1 egg, well beaten
cheese, grated
oil for deep frying
lemon juice and paprika pepper

Wash the brains under cold water, discard skin and membranes. Leave in iced water until white and firm and free from blood, changing the water twice. Cut the brains into pieces the size of a walnut, roll in seasoned flour, beaten egg and grated cheese and fry in deep smoking-hot oil. Drain on absorbent paper and serve hot sprinkled with lemon juice and paprika pepper.

Hot Liver Kebabs

CIĞER TAVASI (Turkey)

all ingredients are as required

liver
milk
olive oil and vinegar marinade (see below)
salt and cayenne pepper
olive oil or other fat for frying
lemon juice

Wash the liver in warm water, if needed cut out any tubes or bits of fat and remove the skin. Cut into small pieces and season with salt and pepper. Prepare a marinade of oil and vinegar, three times more oil than vinegar, and leave the liver in this for 3 hours. Drain the liver and fry quickly in hot oil. Serve hot lightly sprinkled with lemon juice.

Fish Salad

SALATIT SAMAK (Lebanon)

For 6

½kg (about 1lb) filleted white fish
salt
225g (½lb) long grain rice
3 tablespoons (3¾ US) olive oil
1 onion, chopped
1 bay leaf
4 filleted anchovies, chopped
1 crisp apple, chopped
1–2 tablespoons stoneless raisins
green olives to taste, stoned and chopped
1–2 tomatoes, sliced
lemon juice

Poach the fish in lightly salted water until tender, drain, cool, skin and flake off all the flesh from the bone. Bring plenty of water, lightly salted, to the boil, dribble in the rice, stir well and boil for 15 minutes. Drain well and put under gently running cold water for a minute or two. Heat the oil, add the onion and bay leaf and cook until the onion is soft and transparent but not brown. Remove the bay leaf. Add the onion to the rice and stir well. Add the fish, anchovies, apple and raisins. Arrange the salad on an oval dish, garnish with olives and tomatoes and sprinkle with lemon juice.

If the raisins are rather dry, plump them up in water for about 20 minutes and pat dry before using.

Smoked Cod's Roe Salad

TARAMASALATA (Greece)

For 4

This used to be made with the pressed dried roe of the grey mullet, but today this is almost as expensive as real caviar, so even Greeks make this popular dish with cod's roe. Among several recipes for it, the following is typical.

225g (½lb) soft white bread, soaked in water
225g (½lb) smoked cod's roe
olive oil and lemon juice

Squeeze the bread until very dry and crumbly. Crumble the cod's roe and combine the two. Gradually add enough olive oil until the mixture is the consistency of a purée, then add enough lemon juice to loosen it.

Mussels Fried in Batter

MIDYE TAVASI (Turkey)

For 4

1kg (2lb) mussels
oil for deep frying
lemon juice

Batter
2 tablespoons (2½ US) flour
1 egg yolk, well beaten
pinch salt
2 teaspoons (2½ US) olive oil
3–4 tablespoons tepid water
1 egg white, stiffly beaten

Scrape the mussels and wash them in several waters. Cook in just enough water to cover until they open. Take from their shells.

Make the batter: mix the flour, egg yolk, salt, oil and water to a paste thick enough to coat the back of a spoon. Fold in the egg white and use immediately.

Heat the oil. Dip the mussels in the batter, then fry quickly in hot oil. Serve hot with a little lemon juice squeezed over them at the last moment.

Cracked Wheat, Mint and Parsley Salad

TABBULEH (Lebanon)

For 4–6

225g (½lb) cracked wheat (burghal)
1 large or 2 small onions, finely chopped
½ cup (⅔ US) finely chopped fresh mint
salt and pepper
1½–2 cups finely chopped parsley
1–2 tomatoes, finely chopped (optional)
4–5 tablespoons olive oil
juice 1 large lemon

Soak the cracked wheat in water for 30 to 60 minutes before using to allow it to expand. Drain and squeeze out as much moisture as possible, then spread out on a cloth to dry. Combine the cracked wheat with the onion, salt and pepper, mixing it with the hands and squeezing the onion in order to extract all its flavour. Add the remaining ingredients and mix thoroughly.

If using tomato, it should be added at the end. Serve in small individual bowls lined with lettuce or cabbage leaves. If you wish to serve this as a main salad, spread it out on a large platter and decorate it with the chopped tomatoes. Extra lettuce or cabbage leaves are served separately to scoop up the salad.

Bread Salad

FATTOUSH (Lebanon and Syria)

For 6

An enjoyable salad which should be made with dry left-over Arab bread, but dry toast may be used instead although the flavour is not quite the same. One of the seasonings which gives the salad its peculiar flavour is *sumac* (see page 20) water (made by crushing *sumac* seeds and steeping them in warm water for 20 minutes and squeezing out the juice). Lemon juice is the best substitute for this.

3–4 thin slices dry toast, or same quantity dry flat Arab bread
½ cup (⅔ US) sumac water or lemon juice
1 romaine or cos lettuce, finely shredded
1 green pepper, chopped
1–2 large tomatoes, chopped coarsely
½ cup (⅔ US) chopped celery or parsley
½ cup (⅔ US) finely chopped fresh mint
2–3 cloves garlic, finely chopped
1 large white onion, finely chopped
salt
½ cup (⅔ US) olive oil

Break the toast or bread into small pieces. Sprinkle with *sumac* water or lemon juice. Add the lettuce, green pepper, tomatoes, celery or parsley, mint and garlic. Sprinkle the onion generously with salt, stir into the salad, thoroughly mixing all the ingredients, then gradually add the olive oil.

Pasties

BÖREKLER (Turkey)

Savoury-filled pasties, sometimes fried, sometimes baked, are popular throughout the Middle East. They come in all shapes and sizes, chubby and large for lunch, slim and elegant for cocktail parties. The Turks call them *börek*, the Greeks *bourekia*, the Lebanese *sambousik*, the Iraqis *borag*, and so on. Among the most popular is the small fried *börek* filled with meat or cheese, then shaped like a cigarette or a small cushion. For *börek* a special pastry is required, in Turkish called *yufka*, and in Greek *phyllo* (see page 18).

Fillings

Cheese filling

PEYNIRLI IÇ (Turkey)

1 egg yolk
225g (½lb) curd cheese
1 tablespoon (1¼ US) finely chopped parsley

Beat the egg yolk into the cheese, then add the parsley and mix well.

Minced Meat Filling

KIYMALI IÇ (Turkey)

a little oil for frying
1 large onion, grated
225g (½lb) minced meat
salt and black pepper to taste

Heat the oil, add the onion, stir well then add the meat, stir again and cook for 5 minutes over a moderate heat. Add salt and pepper, cover the pan and continue cooking over a low heat for 15 minutes. Cool before using.

Pastry Puffs

PUF BÖREĞI (Turkey)

10–15 sheets phyllo or yufka pastry

Cut the pastry into triangles and on each piece place a little filling, either will do. Dampen the edges with water, fold over the pastry, press down firmly and fry in deep smoking-hot olive oil. Serve hot.

Cigarettes

SIGARA BÖREĞI (Turkey)

Cut the pastry into rectangles, about 7 × 10cm ($2\frac{1}{2}$–$3\frac{1}{2}$in.). Brush each piece with beaten egg, add some cheese filling and roll up like a cigarette. Fry in deep hot olive oil. Serve hot.

Egg Dishes

Eggs are plentiful in the East Mediterranean, especially in the Middle East. In Greece one finds eggs combined with lemon juice to make egg and lemon sauces, or used as a garnish for soups, while coloured hard-boiled eggs are an Easter-tide event. In Turkey eggs are an invaluable ingredient in their cooking. Generally egg dishes are not served at breakfast but at luncheon, with a salad, sliced tomatoes and spring onions. During Ramadan a dish of fried eggs and onions is one of the dishes served to break the month-long fast each day between sun-up and sun-down. In Arab villages eggs deep fried in olive oil are served with Arab bread, pickles, spring onions, chopped mint, fresh marjoram and a salad.

Hard-boiled eggs also are served in a number of ways. My Lebanese cook boiled eggs in our stews and stocks because, she explained, their flavours penetrated the egg shells and gave the hard-boiled eggs an extra flavour.

Omelettes, called *iggah* or *eggah*, are popular throughout the area, not the light, thin omelette of the French but more akin to the thick *frittata* of Italy. They are flavoured with herbs, parsley being a favourite, and fried in olive oil, or vegetable shortening. In the Lebanon there are frying-pans with twelve or so depressions in the surface into which beaten egg is poured and fried to make small omelettes.

Iran has carried the cult of the thick omelette to even greater lengths to make what are called 'egg pies', usually baked but also cooked on top of the stove. These so-called pies are made with a variety of ingredients, usually fresh vegetables which are bound together with eggs.

For the Israelis, eggs are not only considered good to eat but also enter into their traditions. For example, Hamine or brown eggs (*qv*) are served on festival days by the Sephardic Jews. Eggs also represent the mystery of life since they are oval and have no 'opening' to them; also they are the symbol of mourning, to commemorate the destruction of the Temple. Finally, like the Turks and the Arabs, the Israelis serve egg dishes after fasting.

Onion Omelette

'AJJA (Iraq)

For 4–6

4 tablespoons (5 US) olive oil
8 eggs
plenty of parsley, finely chopped
salt and pepper
2 medium-sized onions, minced

Heat the oil in a large omelette pan. Beat the eggs and mix with the remaining ingredients. Pour this mixture into the pan and cook until the underside is firm. Put the pan under the grill and cook until the top is firm and a golden brown.

If fresh parsley is not available, use dried instead. Serve hot: or cold as a sandwich filling.

Walnut and Chive Omelette

KUKU SABZY (Iran)

For 4

6 eggs
pinch saffron, soaked in water
handful chives, finely chopped
30g (1oz/¼ cup US) currants
85g (3oz/2 cups US) soft breadcrumbs
60g (2oz/½ cup US) walnuts, chopped
turmeric to taste
salt and pepper
butter or olive oil for frying

Lightly beat the eggs and combine with the rest of the ingredients, except butter or olive oil. Heat enough butter in a large pan to cover the bottom, add the egg mixture and fry for 5 minutes over a moderate heat. Cut the omelette into four, turn the pieces and cook the other side. Serve straight from the pan.

Or when the omelette is done underneath, it can be put under the grill to brown the top.

Spinach Omelette

IJ-JIT SABAN-EGH (Middle East)

For 2–4

½kg (about 1lb) spinach
4 eggs
salt and pepper
garlic, crushed (optional)
butter or olive oil for frying

Thoroughly wash the spinach and cook without water until tender. Squeeze out all the liquid and finely chop. Lightly beat the eggs, add salt and pepper, combine with the spinach and garlic (if using). Heat just enough butter or oil to cover the bottom of a small frying-pan, pour in the egg and spinach mixture, cover the pan and cook over a gentle heat until set. The omelette should be thick and cut into wedges for serving.

Leek Omelette

EGGAH BI KORRAT (Egypt)

For 6

½kg (about 1lb) leeks
2–3 tablespoons oil for frying
1 teaspoon (1¼ US) sugar
salt and pepper
juice 1 lemon
6 eggs

Wash the leeks, cut away any spoiled leaves and tough ends and slice the rest into rings. Heat the oil, add the leeks, stir well, add the sugar, salt, pepper and lemon juice and cook gently until the leeks are soft and a light golden brown. Take from the stove and cool. Beat the eggs in a bowl, add the leeks with the sauce and stir well. Turn into a greased casserole and bake in a moderate oven (180C, 350F, Mark 4) for 40 to 45 minutes, or fry in a greased frying-pan on top of the stove until set. Serve cut into thick wedges.

Courgettes with Eggs

BAYD BI KUSA (Lebanon)

For 4

6 small courgettes
4 eggs
pinch ground cinnamon (optional)
salt and pepper
30g (1oz/2 tablespoons US) butter or oil

Wash, thinly peel and thickly slice the courgettes. Cook in a little water until soft and drain well. Beat the eggs, add salt and pepper. Put the courgettes in the bottom of a shallow, well greased casserole, pour the beaten egg over the top, sprinkle with cinnamon and bake in a hot oven (220C, 425F, Mark 7) until the eggs have set. Garnish with a little melted butter or hot oil and serve at once.

Eggs with Onions

YUMURTA SOĞANLI (Turkey)

For 2–4

60g (2oz/4 tablespoons US) butter or olive oil
4 medium-sized onions, thickly sliced
4 eggs
$\frac{1}{4}$ cup ($\frac{1}{2}$ US) milk
salt and pepper
parsley to taste, chopped

Heat the butter in a large frying-pan, add the onions and cook over a low heat until they are soft but not brown. Carefully slide in the eggs on top of the onions, add the milk, salt and pepper and continue cooking until the eggs are set. Sprinkle generously with parsley and serve immediately.

Minced Meat with Eggs

KIYMALI YUMURTA (Turkey)

For 3–6

30g (1oz/2 tablespoons US) oil or butter
225g (½lb) minced meat
1 large onion, grated
1 teaspoon (1¼ US) black pepper
salt to taste
6 eggs

Heat the oil in a frying-pan, add the minced meat, spread it round the pan with a fork, then add the onion and cook over a moderate heat, stirring frequently until the meat is crumbly. Cover the pan and continue cooking until all the moisture from the meat has been absorbed. Add the pepper and salt, stir well, then hollow-out six depressions in the mixture and drop an egg carefully in each. Cover the pan and continue cooking for 3 or 4 minutes, or until the eggs are set.

Eggs on Tomatoes

DOMATESLI YUMURTA (Turkey)

For 3–6

4 large tomatoes
1–2 medium-sized onions, finely chopped
a little oil or other fat
salt and pepper
6 eggs

Blanch, peel and chop the tomatoes. Heat enough oil in a frying-pan to cover the bottom, add the onion(s), stir and fry for 3 minutes, then add the tomatoes. Cook gently for 15 minutes, stirring from time to time; add salt and pepper. Lower the heat and continue cooking until the tomatoes are soft. Slide in the eggs, one by one, on top of the tomatoes being careful not to break them. Cook slowly until the whites are set and the yolks still soft. Prick the yolks with a knitting needle and let the yolks spread out and mingle with the tomatoes and egg whites. Serve at once.

'Scrambled' Eggs

CHATCHOUKA, CHECHOUKA or TETCHOUKA
(Middle East)

For 3–4

This dish of eggs is of Tunisian origin but popular throughout the Middle East, including Israel.

2 small green peppers
oil
2 onions, diced
1 small chilli pepper (optional)
salt and pepper
2 cloves garlic, crushed
6–8 tomatoes, peeled and halved
6–8 eggs

Cut the peppers into halves, take out cores and seeds, then cut the flesh into thin strips. Heat a few tablespoons of oil in a deep frying-pan, add the onions, peppers, and chilli pepper, sprinkle with salt, pepper and garlic and cook gently until soft. Add the tomatoes and cook until these are soft. Break the eggs into the pan and continue cooking until they are set, or if preferred the eggs can be gently stirred into the mixture until it becomes thick and creamy. Add salt and pepper and serve hot.

Poached Eggs in Yogurt

YUMURTA ÇILBIR (Turkey)

For 6

4 cups (5 US) yogurt
2–4 cloves garlic, crushed
salt
1 dessertspoon (1 tablespoon US) vinegar
6 eggs
30g (1oz/2 tablespoons US) butter
paprika pepper

Beat the yogurt, flavour it with garlic, salt and vinegar, then divide into six small bowls. Poach the eggs and drop one into each bowl, taking care not to break them. Melt the butter in a pan and add enough paprika pepper to colour it a deep red. Garnish each bowl with this dressing and serve.

Egg and Vegetable Pie

KUKUYE SABZI (Iran)

For 6

2–3 leeks, chopped
225g ($\frac{1}{2}$lb) spinach or chard, chopped
$\frac{1}{2}$ small lettuce, chopped
small bunch spring onions, chopped
12 walnuts, chopped
1 cup ($1\frac{1}{4}$ US) cooked, canned or frozen peas
30g (1oz/$\frac{1}{4}$ cup US) flour
salt and pepper to taste
8 eggs
60g (2oz/$\frac{1}{4}$ cup US) butter
yogurt

Mix the first six ingredients in a bowl. Add the flour, salt and pepper and mix thoroughly. Beat the eggs, pour into the bowl and mix well. Melt the butter in a 23cm (9in) cake pan and rub it round the sides. Add the vegetable and egg mixture and bake in a pre-heated moderate oven (180C, 350F, Mark 4) until set, about 1 hour. Serve hot or cold with yogurt.

This pie turns out easily, like a cake, but if it is to be served cold, leave it to cool before taking it from the pan.

Egg Kebabs

AIJET BEYTHAT (Middle East)

hard-boiled eggs, as required
oil for frying
salt, pepper, ground cinnamon and turmeric mixed, all to taste

Shell the eggs and prick them through the white all over to just reach the yolk. This prevents splitting and helps the flavours penetrate, also it gives to the eggs a slightly spongey texture. Combine the spices and mix well. Heat a little oil in a small pan, add the eggs, lower the heat and fry them until brown all over, turning them repeatedly. Take the eggs from the pan and, while still hot, roll in the mixed spices and serve hot with vegetables or meat.

Hard-Boiled Eggs

BEID HAMINE (Middle East)

It was in Istanbul where I was introduced to these eggs by my Turco-Greek cook. She used to put a large number of eggs into a big pan with water, add Turkish coffee grounds and the brown outer leaves of onions, then cover the top with a thin layer of olive oil, which prevented the water from evaporating. The pan was then put on the top of our solid fuel stove and left overnight. When the eggs were shelled, the whites were *café-au-lait* in colour, the yolks almost saffron and creamy in texture, and the flavour was vaguely of chestnuts.

However, this method of cooking eggs is neither Turkish nor Greek but comes from the Sephardic Jewish community. Although the eggs can be served among the starters, it is more usual to serve them as a garnish for meat stews and, in particular, for *Foul Madumnas* (see page 31). Failing a solid fuel stove, the eggs can be hard-boiled and then pressure-cooked for 1½ hours with almost as good results, or even baked for hours in a very slow oven (80C, 175F, Mark ¼).

Cereal Dishes

There are reputedly 7,000 different types of rice, differing slightly from field to field as grapes do from vineyard to vineyard. These differences, although important to growers, do not enter into the calculations of Eastern rice eaters, let alone the Western buyer. However, in rice-eating countries the choosing of rice for the various dishes is important. The function of rice is that of an important main dish to which can be added either a number of other dishes, or served with sauces, more particularly in Iran. All rice-eating people have different ideas on how to cook rice. Some wash it, others do not. The Iranians wash rice, even soak it for hours to produce their particular pilaus. Others always wash it well and soak it for 30 minutes or so. However, packaged rice does not require such treatment.

Generally rice can be divided into long, medium and short grain types. In long grain rice the grains are 4 to 5 times as long as they are wide. When cooked, the grains will separate and the rice look fluffy and light. This rice is preferred for pilaus. Also it can be allowed to get cold and be used in salads.

The shorter, plumper grains of the medium and short types cook tender and moist but tend to stick together. These types are used in the Mediterranean region for sweet puddings and risottos.

There are, we are told, as many different pilaus as there are stars in the sky. Pilaus are made from rice, usually long grain, also from cracked wheat (*burghal*). Whatever the type of pilau, its essential quality is that it should be light and fluffy. It can be plain, savoury or sweet. A light, plain pilau topped with a large pat of butter is excellent. Pilaus take their name from the main ingredient with which they are flavoured, *ie*, *iç pilau*, or Turkish chicken liver pilau. Apart from the many varieties of pilau in the region, there are almost as many different ways of spelling pilau.

Rice with Lemon Sauce

RUZ OU HAMUD (Egypt)

For 6–8

To prepare the *hamud* or sauce:
bones, neck, head, feet, giblets, wing bones, etc. of a chicken
1 medium-sized turnip, coarsely chopped
1 large potato, coarsely chopped
1–2 stalks celery, coarsely chopped
1–2 tablespoons chopped parsley
salt and pepper
1 small onion, chopped (optional)
juice 2 lemons

To prepare the rice:
½kg (about 1lb) long grain rice
1½ tablespoons (1¾ US) oil

Put the sauce ingredients into a pan with 4 cups (5 US) of water. Bring to the boil and continue boiling for about 10 minutes, then lower the heat and cook gently until the vegetables have disintegrated and are mushy. Take out the chicken bones, etc. and discard, although the giblets can be chopped and returned to the pan.

While the sauce is cooking, prepare the rice. Bring 2 cups ($2\frac{1}{2}$ US) of salted water to the boil, add the rice and oil, lower the heat to simmering, half cover the pan and cook for 15 minutes, stirring from time to time with a fork. Uncover and leave the rice for 10 minutes over the *lowest* possible heat.

Serve the rice and its sauce separately, pouring a ladleful of sauce over each portion of rice when serving.

In Egypt this dish is served almost every day of the week, usually after the meat course.

Plain Pilau

PILÂV SADE (Turkey)

For 6

8 tablespoons ($\frac{1}{2}$ cup US) olive oil
$\frac{1}{2}$kg (about 1 lb) long grain rice
salt and black pepper to taste
4 cups (5 US) boiling meat stock
butter

Heat the oil in a large pan, add the rice and cook it for 5 minutes, stirring all the while to prevent sticking. Add salt and pepper, then gradually the boiling stock, stir, cover the pan with a cloth, then tightly with the lid. Cook over the *lowest* possible heat for 30 minutes until the rice is tender and all the liquid absorbed. Turn off the heat but leave the pan on the stove, covered, for 15 minutes by which time the rice will be dry and each grain separate. Stir in some butter or turn out the rice on to a large serving dish and garnish it with butter.

With this basic pilau a variety of garnishes can be served. For example, fried tomatoes or onions, or fried chicken, chicken livers, lamb kebabs or small rissoles, even cubes of fried fish, etc.

Pilau

IÇ PILÂV (Turkey)

For 6

225g ($\frac{1}{2}$lb) calves' liver
110g ($\frac{1}{4}$lb) butter
3 onions, finely chopped
30g (1oz/$\frac{1}{4}$ cup US) pine-nuts
$\frac{1}{2}$kg (about 1lb) long grain rice
salt and black pepper
2 teaspoons ($2\frac{1}{2}$ US) sugar
$\frac{1}{2}$ teaspoon ($\frac{2}{3}$ US) mixed spice
60g (2oz/$\frac{1}{2}$ cup US) currants
2 tomatoes, peeled and chopped
4 cups (5 US) boiling meat stock or water
fresh sage, parsley and/or mint

Wash the liver, cut out any bits of fat and tubes, and chop it into small pieces. Melt the butter and lightly fry the liver. Take it from the pan, put aside but keep hot. In the same pan fry the onions until soft but not brown. Add the nuts and finally the rice. Fry this for 5 minutes, stirring all the time to prevent sticking. Add the seasonings, sugar, spice, currants, tomatoes and gradually the hot liquid. Stir again, cover the pan with a cloth, clamp on the lid and cook gently for 30 minutes until all the liquid is absorbed. When the pilau is dry, return the liver to the pan on top of the rice, sprinkle lightly with herbs, re-cover the pan and leave for 15 minutes on a warm stove.

Turn out on to a large, warm platter to serve.

Steamed Rice

CHELO (Iran)

For 6

The two main methods of cooking rice in Iran are *chelo* and *polo*. The first, which is plain boiled rice, is eaten only at lunch and the name is applied to those rice dishes in which the rice is cooked in water with seasoning, and over which a *khoresh* (sauce) or kebabs are served. *Polo* is the name given to rice which is cooked together with other ingredients, *i.e.* meat, fruit or vegetables.

When cooking *chelo*, the rice at the bottom of the pan is deliberately allowed to form a crisp crust called *tah dig*, or *hakkakah* in Arabic. This is scraped up and served as a garnish.

½kg (about 1lb) long grain rice
rock or very coarse salt to taste
110g (4oz/½ cup US) butter

Wash the rice two or three times in lukewarm water and soak it overnight in enough cold water to reach a level of at least 6cm (3in) above the rice. Add a large quantity of salt tied in a cloth (if the salt is loose, say the Iranians, the starch comes away from the rice and breaks it up). Next morning put at least 2½l (4½ pints/5¼ US) of water in a large pan and boil until it bubbles. Dribble in the rice so that the water is boiling all the time and the rice bobs up and down. Cook for 10 minutes or until the rice is soft but not yet tender. Stir with a wooden spoon once or twice to prevent the grains from sticking together. Drain well in a sieve and rinse in lukewarm water.

In the same pan in which you have cooked the rice, melt the butter, add 2 cups (2½ US) of lukewarm water and bring this to the boil. Take out half of the butter-water and put aside. Sprinkle the rice back into the pan in such a way that it makes a loose cone shape which allows the steam to reach every grain of rice. Cook quickly for 1 minute over a good heat to let some rice stick to the bottom of the pan. Now add the remaining butter-water, distributing it evenly, cover the pan with a cloth, clamp on the lid and leave the pan over a very low heat for 30 to 40 minutes. The rice on the bottom of the pan will form a thick brown and crisp crust while the rest remains white and fluffy.

Turn out the rice and serve it on a large platter. Scrape the bottom of the pan and take off the crust in large chunks. These are served on separate plates or as a garnish.

Chelo rice is served with sauces (see pages 62–71), and of course with *chelo kebab* (see page 154).

A drink of lightly salted yogurt, diluted with water, called *Abdug*, is always served with *chelo*.

Chicken or **Sweet Pilau**

SHIRINI POLO (Iran)

For 8–10

This particular *polo* is a special favourite with the Iranians, 'their wedding dish par excellence'. It should be made, they say, with a chicken 'as tender as a poem', and with rice from the paddy fields of the Caspian Sea region.

225g (½lb) carrots
2 tablespoons (2½ US) sugar
peel ½ orange, shredded
85g (3oz/1 cup US) blanched almonds, slivered
1 medium-sized chicken
salt and pepper
½kg (about 1lb) long grain rice
110g (4oz/½ cup US) butter
1 teaspoon (1¼ US) saffron or turmeric

Scrape and grate the carrots. Put into a pan with the sugar, orange peel, almonds and a little water and cook gently until the carrots are tender. Poach the chicken in a little water with salt and pepper added until just tender. Take from the pan and cut into serving pieces, or strip the meat from the bone; this makes for easier serving and eating.

While the chicken is cooking, prepare the rice in the same manner as for *chelo* (see page 54) to the point of rinsing it in warm water. Melt the butter, add a cup (1¼ US) of lukewarm water. Pour half of this into a large pan, stir well, add a layer of rice, cover this with the carrot mixture, add another layer of rice, then the chicken, and finally add the rest of the rice. Pour the remainder of the butter-water over the top, distributing it evenly. Stretch a cloth across the top of the pan, cover with the lid and leave over the lowest possible heat for 30 to 40 minutes. Mix the saffron with about a tablespoonful of water; when the rice is ready, take out about 6 tablespoonfuls, mix with the saffron, return to the pan and lightly mix into the rest of the rice.

Turn out to serve on a hot platter.

Rice, Chicken and Onions

RIZE BIL FARARIZE (Middle East)

For 6–8

½kg (about 1lb) long grain rice
1 large chicken, jointed
salt
110g (4oz/½ cup US) butter or other fat
½kg (about 1lb) onions, finely chopped
ground cinnamon, nutmeg and cumin to taste

Soak the rice in cold water for 1 hour and drain. Rub the chicken well with salt. Heat the butter in a large pan, add the onions and fry these until they change colour. Add the chicken pieces and fry until they are brown on both sides. Add water to cover and cook gently until the chicken is tender. Strain off the liquid from the chicken, pour this into another pan adding sufficient hot water to have at least 2 cups (2½ US) of liquid. Bring this to the boil, add the rice and cook until the rice is tender, adding salt and spices just before it is ready. Drain and dry for a few minutes in a warm oven. Turn out the rice on to a large hot platter and garnish with the chicken and onions.

Chestnut Pilau and Meat

MAQLUB EL ABUFARWA (Iraq)

For 6–8

225g (½lb) long grain rice
½kg (about 1lb) chestnuts
½kg (about 1lb) lamb or mutton
salt and pepper
110g (4oz/½ cup US) butter or oil
4 cups (5 US) water

Wash the rice and soak it in hot water for 30 minutes. Cut a slit in each of the chestnuts and cook them in boiling water until their inner and outer skins are easily removed, between 10 and 20 minutes, according to their freshness. Wipe the meat with a damp cloth and cut into pieces approximately the same size as the chestnuts. Put the meat into a pan with just enough water to cover, add salt and pepper and simmer until the water has evaporated. Heat the butter, add the pieces of meat and fry until brown all over. Add the chestnuts and water. Bring to the boil. Drain the rice, add this to the pan, boil for 2 minutes, then lower the heat, cover the pan and continue to cook for 15 minutes. Leave for 30 minutes over the lowest possible heat.

Turn out to serve hot as a main dish.

Fruit Pilau

MIVEH TAZEH POLO (Iran)

For 6–8

½kg (about 1lb) long grain rice
salt to taste
½kg (about 1lb) fresh fruit
sugar to taste
2–3 tablespoons butter or other fat

Cook the rice in 8 cups (10 US) of boiling salted water for 20 minutes or until quite soft. Cook the fruit in sugar and water until soft. Heat the butter in a fairly large pan, add a layer of rice, then fruit and continue in this manner until the rice and fruit are used up. Cover the pan with a cloth and a tightly fitting lid and leave over a low heat, preferably over an asbestos mat, for 30 minutes.

Turn out on to a large dish and serve as a main or sweet dish. Any type of fruit which can be cooked may be used in this pilau.

Date and Lentil Pilau

ADDAS POLO (Iran)

For 8–10

½kg (about 1lb) long grain rice
170g (6oz/1 cup US) lentils
225g (½lb/1 cup US) butter
1 small onion, finely chopped
110g (¼lb) dried apricots, chopped
225g (½lb) dates, stoned
60g (2oz/scant ½ cup US) blanched almonds, chopped
85g (3oz/½ cup US) raisins or sultanas

Prepare and cook the rice as for *chelo* (see page 54) to the point of rinsing it with lukewarm water. Cook the lentils until soft. Melt half the butter and combine with 1 cup (1¼ US) of lukewarm water. Put aside but keep warm. Heat the rest of the butter and lightly fry the onion until it changes colour, then add the dates, apricots, almonds and raisins. Put aside. Put half the butter-water in a large pan, add a layer of a third of the rice, then one of half the lentils, another third of rice, then the dried fruits, etc. and finally the rest of the lentils, the rice and butter-water, distributing the latter evenly. Cover the pan first with a cloth, then with the lid and cook for 30 to 40 minutes over the lowest possible heat. Turn out to serve on a large hot platter as a main dish.

Esau's Mess of Potage

MUJADDARAH (Middle East)

For 6

There are as many ways of spelling the name of this popular Middle East dish as there are different ways to prepare it.

2 cups ($2\frac{1}{2}$ US) large dark lentils
8 cups (10 US) water
$\frac{1}{2}$ cup ($\frac{2}{3}$ US) long grain rice
salt to taste
4 tablespoons (5 US) olive oil
2 onions, chopped
2 onions, thickly sliced

Soak the lentils overnight in cold water (see below). Drain and put them in a large pan with the water and cook over a moderate heat until they are almost tender. Add the rice and salt and continue cooking until both the rice and lentils are tender. Heat half the oil, add the chopped onions and fry until brown; mix these into the lentils and rice and, with the pan uncovered, simmer for 5 minutes, stirring from time to time to prevent sticking. While the lentils and rice are cooking, heat the remaining oil and fry the sliced onions to a dark brown. Serve the lentils and rice on a large platter garnished with the fried, sliced onions.

Not all lentils require such long pre-soaking; consult the instructions printed on the packet.

Cracked Wheat Pilau

BURGHAL PILAF (Lebanon)

For 6–8

110g (4oz/½ cup US) butter or margarine
½kg (about 1lb) cracked wheat
1 medium-sized onion, chopped
salt and pepper
¾l (1¼ pints/3 cups US) boiling meat stock

Melt half the butter in a pan, add the cracked wheat, stir it well and cook for 10 minutes. Melt the remaining butter in another pan and fry the onion until soft and yellow. Add to the cracked wheat, stir well, add salt and pepper then the stock and stir again. Cover the pan and cook over a low heat for another 10 minutes, or until the cracked wheat has absorbed all the liquid. Uncover the pan and test the cracked wheat. Should it seem a little dry (not very likely), add a little more liquid.

The pilau can be served with melted butter, fried onions, a tomato sauce, with fried sliced peppers or aubergines, fried pine-nuts, etc.

Sauces

We are told that it was the Greeks who invented sauces, as they did many other dishes. Orion, one of the seven sages of the culinary arts, is credited with the invention of the white sauce, while another introduced the brown sauce to the world. We learn further that the ancient Greek poet Menander invented a fish sauce of such excellence that its fame has passed down through the ages, but the recipe has been lost so we shall never know whether this fame was justified.

But the Greeks have gone on inventing sauces, not in quantity but in quality. Without question the national sauce is *Saltsa Avgolemono* (*qv*), egg and lemon sauce, although almost as important are the garlic sauces, like *Skorthalia* (*qv*) of which there are several versions. Most Greek sauces are made with bread, nuts, garlic, potatoes, and naturally olive oil and lemon juice, plus tomatoes and other vegetables, but almost never thickened with flour.

The Turks strongly favour egg and lemon sauces, also those made with yogurt, which are either hot or cold and flavoured with garlic, and often garnished with a hot butter and paprika flavoured dressing. Like the Greeks, they have a number of nut sauces, such as *Tarator Çamfistikli* (*qv*), and their own version of a pungent garlic sauce, *Tarator Sade* (*qv*). Also found in Turkey are many of the usual sauces, béchamel, hollandaise, tarragon, etc., which they have taken over from the French but made their own with a slight difference here and there.

In the Arab world we find different but good sauces, although with not such variety. Here the most favoured sauce is *Tarator Bi Tahina* (*qv*) which is often served with grilled meats or with fish. In Iraq many sauces are simply made from the thickened liquid of stews or ragoûts, resulting from long cooking, and then flavoured with tomato concentrate.

Iran has given great importance to the making of sauces which are almost stews or ragoûts and always served with rice. This makes them almost a dish in themselves. Such sauces are eaten daily and are delightful combinations of meat, poultry, game, vegetables and fruits, the combination depending on the season and/or the imagination of the cook. They are not hot sauces, indeed, the usual spicings are mild and quite often rose-water is added. Many of the *khoresh* recipes are traditional and housewives will prepare a *chelo khoresh* for a luncheon whatever else she may be serving. If there is a secret in the preparation of these sauces, it lies in their seasoning and blending.

In Israel we find most of the usual international sauces plus some which are new to many in the West. There is one which is made from finely crushed fenugreek seeds, flavoured with garlic, hot spices and tomatoes. It comes from the Yemeni Jewish immigrants but is of Arab origin and is claimed to make women plump and fertile as well as horses fleet-footed, an odd combination, I feel, but there it is. There are other sauces, rather fiery and heavily garlicked, but the Israelis, like their Arab neighbours, share a passion for all of the *tahina* sauces.

Throughout the region dressings for salads are made with olive oil and generally lemon juice, although one does meet dressings made with wine vinegar. Crushed garlic is frequently added and rather more lemon juice is used in proportion to oil than in a French dressing.

Béchamel Sauce

BECHAMEL

30g (1oz/2 tablespoons US) butter
30g (1oz/¼ cup US) flour
1 cup (1¼ US) hot water, milk or stock
salt and pepper

Heat half the butter in a small pan, add the flour and stir well. Cook for 1 minute. Gradually add the liquid, stirring all the while, and cook for 10 minutes. Add the remainder of the butter, stir until this has melted into the sauce, add salt and pepper and beat well.

Egg and Lemon Sauce

AVGOLEMONO (Greece)

2–3 eggs
2 cups (2½ US) hot stock
½ cup (⅔ US) strained lemon juice

The stock must match the dish with which the sauce is to be served, *i.e.* chicken stock with a chicken dish, vegetable stock if serving the sauce with boiled cabbage, and fish stock with a fish dish.

Beat the eggs until light in colour, slowly add the lemon juice, beating constantly. Gradually add the hot stock and whisk well. Heat the sauce until hot but do not allow it to boil or it will curdle. Serve in soups, with *dolmas*, with meat balls, fish, or chicken, etc.

Garlic Sauce with Breadcrumbs

SKORTHALIA ME YALETTA (Greece)

6–8 cloves garlic
salt
2 cups ($2\frac{1}{2}$ US) breadcrumbs
$\frac{3}{4}$ cup (1 US) olive oil
juice 1 lemon

Pound the garlic with about 1 teaspoonful of salt. Add the breadcrumbs and pound to a paste. Alternately, gradually add the olive oil and lemon juice until you have a sauce of the same consistency as mayonnaise.

Garlic Sauce

TARATOR SADE (Turkey)

4–6 cloves garlic
1 teaspoon ($1\frac{1}{4}$ US) salt
2 tablespoons ($2\frac{1}{2}$ US) olive oil
lemon juice

Crush and pound the garlic with the salt until pulpy. Gradually add half the olive oil until it is absorbed into the garlic, then add the rest slowly to produce a thick sauce. Add a few drops of lemon juice to thin it to the required consistency, *i.e.* like a thin mayonnaise.

Use with cold meats and especially fish and plain boiled potatoes.

Garlic and Egg Sauce

SALÇA YUMURTALI (Turkey)

4 cloves garlic
1 teaspoon (1¼ US) salt
2 egg yolks
1 cup (1¼ US) olive oil
1 tablespoon (1¼ US) lemon juice

Crush the garlic and pound with salt in a mortar until pulpy. Beat in the egg yolks and add the olive oil drop by drop as for mayonnaise. Loosen with a few drops of lemon juice.

If using a blender, put the egg yolks, salt and (chopped) garlic in the blender and mix for one minute at high speed. At the same speed pour in the oil at a trickle until the sauce has thickened, then add the lemon juice and blend for a few seconds.

Use with fish, especially cold white fish, or with plain boiled potatoes. Very similar to *ailloli*.

Garlic and Tahina Sauce

TARATOR BI TAHINA (Middle East)

1 cup (1¼ US) tahina (see page 20)
warm water
juice 1 lemon
4–6 cloves garlic or to taste
salt

Put the *tahina* into a bowl and gradually add warm water and lemon juice alternately to make a thick and creamy sauce with the consistency of a mayonnaise. Crush the garlic with a little salt and work this mixture into the *tahina*.

The sauce can be served in small individual dishes, sprinkled with finely chopped parsley and cayenne pepper, and taken as a dip with soft brown bread, or served with fish, as is done by the fishermen along the Mediterranean coasts.

Hazel-Nut Sauce

MARAKIT BUNDUK (Iraq)

1 thick slice white bread, crustless
225g ($\frac{1}{2}$lb) roasted hazel-nuts
1 clove garlic, crushed
1 tablespoon ($1\frac{1}{4}$ US) lemon juice
salt
chicken stock
paprika pepper

Soak the bread and squeeze it dry. Chop the nuts; mix with the bread and garlic and either mince or blend. Add the lemon juice, salt to taste and just enough warm stock to make a thick but flowing sauce. Add enough paprika to give it a pale pink colour.

Use with chicken and boiled meats.

Pine-Nut Sauce

TARATOR ÇAMFISTIKLI (Turkey)

110g (4oz/1 cup US) pine-nuts
2 cloves garlic
1 teaspoon ($1\frac{1}{4}$US) salt
olive oil
lemon juice or vinegar

Crush the pine-nuts in a blender or put through the finest blade of a mincer. Crush the garlic with the salt until pulpy. Combine the garlic and pine-nuts and pound until thoroughly mixed. Gradually add enough olive oil, drop by drop, beating all the while, until you have a thick smooth sauce. Thin this down with lemon juice.

Alternatively, put the nuts, garlic and salt in a blender, whisk until pulverized, add about 1 tablespoonful of oil to make a smooth sauce, and a little lemon juice to thin it.

Use with fish, cold meats, chicken and turkey.

Herb Sauce

SALKHA (Lebanon)

Either British or American spoons may be used in this recipe.

6–8 tablespoons olive oil
½ teaspoon each salt, cayenne pepper and dry mustard
3–4 tablespoons tarragon vinegar
½ teaspoon each finely chopped: chives, tarragon, spring onion, parsley, chervil, gherkin
½ teaspoon icing sugar

Mix the oil, salt, pepper and mustard, then gradually add the vinegar, stirring vigorously all the time. Add the remaining ingredients, a little at a time, stirring well after each addition. Stir well and put aside in a cool place for 12 hours. Strain through a hair sieve before serving.

Use with cold meat, poultry and fish.

Yogurt Sauce

SALÇA YOĞURT (Turkey)

Well-beaten thick yogurt, seasoned with salt and pepper. Sometimes a little tomato paste is added to give a light colouring, but not enough to interfere with the yogurt flavour.

Use with hot vegetable dishes, ragoûts, etc.

Vegetable Sauce

KHORESH QORMEH SABZI (Iran)

110g (4oz/½ cup US) butter or margarine
1 large onion, chopped
½kg (about 1lb) lamb, cut into cubes
170g (6oz/1 cup US) yellow split peas
2 leeks, chopped
225g (½lb) spinach, finely chopped
handful parsley, chopped
salt and pepper
2–3 tablespoons lemon juice
ground cinnamon to taste
½ teaspoon (⅔ US) turmeric

Melt half the butter in a large pan, add the onion and fry until it begins to change colour; add the meat, stirring it well into the onion. Add 2 cups (2½ US) of water and the split peas and cook over a low heat until the meat is tender. Melt the remainder of the butter in another pan, add the leeks, spinach, parsley, salt and pepper and cook this mixture, stirring from time to time until it becomes dark and fragrant. Add this to the simmering meat, then the lemon juice, cinnamon and turmeric and continue to cook for about 20 minutes. Serve with *chelo* rice.

Often used in this sauce is the green leaf of the fenugreek plant which gives it a distinct but slightly bitter flavour. Also, when in season, chopped spring onions are used, or, instead of split peas, black-eyed peas or dried haricot beans, previously soaked and parboiled, are used. Failing lemon juice, a wine or cider vinegar does as well.

Apple and Meat Sauce

KHORESH SIB (Iran)

For 6

110g (4oz/½ cup US) butter
1 large onion, chopped
½kg (about 1lb) lamb, cut into cubes
juice 1 lemon
salt, pepper and ground cinnamon to taste
4 large firm tart apples

Melt half the butter in a large pan, add the onion and fry until soft and beginning to change colour. Take from the pan, sprinkle with a little lemon juice, put aside and keep warm. Add the meat to the same pan, sprinkle with the remainder of the lemon juice and fry, turning the meat frequently until the pieces are browned. Add about 2 cups of warm water, salt, pepper and cinnamon, stir well and cook over a low heat until the meat is tender. Peel, core and thickly slice the apples, then cut each slice into half to make crescent or half-moon shapes. Heat the remaining butter and gently simmer the apples until they begin to change colour, are soft but still firm. Return the onions to the pan with the meat, stir gently to mix, then add the apples, arranging the pieces carefully on top of the sauce. Simmer for 5 to 10 minutes, merely to combine the flavours, then serve on top of a mound of *chelo* or plain boiled rice.

Popular variations using fruits other than apples:

KHORESH ALU: prunes, soaked, stoned, drained and added to the sauce 20 minutes before it is ready.
KHORESH HOLU: peaches, peeled and stoned, cut into wedges then treated exactly as the apples.
KHORESH RIVAS: coarsely chopped rhubarb added to the sauce at the same time as the seasonings, cooked until soft but not mushy.

Orange Sauce

KHORESH PORTAGAL (Iran)

60g (2oz/4 tablespoons US) cooking fat
1kg (2¼lb) meat, cut into small pieces
1 cup (1¼ US) warm water
salt, pepper, paprika pepper to taste
1 large onion, finely chopped
30g (1oz/2 tablespoons US) butter
1–2 tablespoons lemon juice
4–5 oranges
110g (4oz/½ cup US) sugar, preferably brown
½ cup (⅔ US) mild vinegar

Heat the cooking fat in a pan and fry the meat until it browns. Add the water and seasonings and cook slowly for 25 to 30 minutes, or until the meat is tender. Heat the butter, add the onion and fry until soft and golden brown; add the lemon juice, stir well, then put aside, off the heat. Peel the oranges, scrape off all pith, divide into segments and remove any pips. Put the oranges into a small pan. Stir the sugar into the vinegar and add this to the oranges and cook over a gentle heat for 15 to 20 minutes. Take out the oranges with a slotted spoon, arrange these alternately with the onions over the top of the still simmering meat. Pour the liquid from the oranges over the top and continue cooking over a low heat until the meat is absolutely tender. Serve over *chelo* or plain boiled rice.

This sauce can be prepared with duck, chicken or lamb.

General Salad Dressing

Either British or American spoons can be used.

3–4 tablespoons olive oil
2 tablespoons lemon juice or wine vinegar
crushed garlic to taste
salt and black pepper

Combine these ingredients. Finely chopped parsley or fresh coriander, and either fresh or dried mint are often added.

Soups

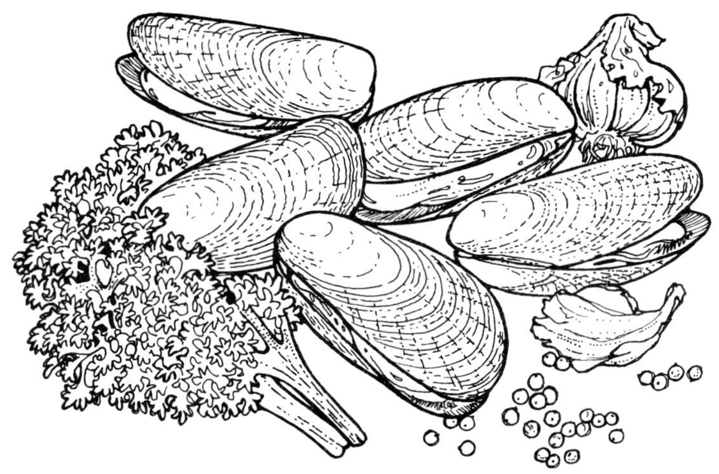

In the preparation of soups there is no doubt that the people of the Middle East are masters, and it is interesting to note how many of the soups are intertwined or are variations on a main theme. The explanation for this in part stems from the love of good food shown by the Turkish sultans and pashas who, wherever they were living, continued to eat as well as they did in their own country. These gourmets sent to Vienna for recipes, they took from the Caucassians, from North Africa, and the Arab peninsular until their repertoire was international. Sometimes the recipe was kept intact, at other times changed, probably because not all the ingredients could be obtained, or they were against Moslem dietary laws. Thus one finds a soup recipe, say in Greece, which appears in a dozen different guises throughout the area with perhaps only slight variations but always claimed as a strictly local dish.

One tends to think of the Middle East as a place of eternal sun, which is far from the case. I have travelled through miles of snowy uplands in East Turkey and in Iran, and been almost frozen in the mountains of the Lebanon, although below the city of Beirut was bathed in sunshine. So one finds thick, warming and satisfying soups which defy the cold, while others are light and easy on jaded appetites.

If there is imagination in the making of starters, there is an equal imagination spent in the making of soups. Not for these cooks a package or a can, no, they start from scratch and they combine meat with fruit, with vegetables, and, when making fish soups, with all the harvest of their local seaboard. In the winter, soups are steaming hot; in the summer more often than not they are iced. Soups are considered worthy to be served on important occasions such as weddings and ceremonial functions. But equally important in the minds of the people is that soups are health-giving and offered to invalids.

Many of the recipes for today's Middle Eastern soups are of ancient origin, some hardly altered although the modern housewife prefers to use modern implements rather than exert the amount of elbow grease demanded in the old days; and the pressure cooker has taken the sting out of that long, slow cooking so necessary for stock making.

As in the West, housewives of the Middle East feel that a good bowl of soup, plus a salad, some bread and cheese followed by fruit is satisfying as a complete family meal.

Egg and Cheese Soup

PEYNIR ÇORBASI YUMURTALI (Turkey)

For 3

2½ cups (3 US) seasoned chicken stock
2 egg yolks
2–3 tablespoons grated sharp cheese

Gently heat the chicken stock. While this is cooking, beat the eggs well and mix with the cheese. Put into a pan and stir over a low heat, using a wooden spoon, until the cheese has melted. Gradually add the stock, still stirring, and continue cooking until the soup is almost boiling: do not let it quite boil as the eggs will curdle.

Egg and Lemon Soup

SOUPA AVGOLEMONO (Greece)

For 4–6

1½l (3 pints/3¾ US) chicken stock
85g (3oz/scant ½ cup US) long grain rice
salt and pepper
2 egg yolks, well beaten
juice 1 lemon

Bring the stock to the boil, add the rice, stir and season and continue to boil for 15 minutes. Lower the heat to simmering. Beat the egg yolks thoroughly, gradually beat in the lemon juice and 2 to 3 tablespoons of the hot stock. Pour this into the soup, stirring all the while. Continue simmering for 2 minutes. Cover the pan and leave the soup without heat for 5 minutes before serving.

Egg and Lemon Fish Soup

BALIK ÇORBASI (Turkey)

For 6

2l ($3\frac{1}{2}$ pints/4 US) fish stock
60g (2 tablespoons/$2\frac{1}{2}$ US) flour
2 whole eggs
juice 1 lemon

Bring the stock to the boil, lower the heat and let it simmer for a few minutes. Mix the flour with water (or milk) to make a thin paste, stir this into the stock and cook gently for 5 minutes. Beat the eggs until frothy, gradually add the lemon juice and 2 to 3 tablespoons of the hot stock, stir this into the stock over the lowest possible heat and continue cooking for two more minutes.

Serve with large *croûtons*.

Mussel Soup

MIDYE ÇORBASI (Turkey)

For 6

2l ($3\frac{1}{2}$ pints/4 US) mussels
1–$1\frac{1}{2}$l ($1\frac{3}{4}$–3 pints/2–$3\frac{3}{4}$ US) water
2 onions, coarsely chopped
3 cloves garlic, chopped
2 tablespoons ($2\frac{1}{2}$ US) flour
milk
pepper, preferably freshly ground
chopped parsley to taste

Scrape the mussels and wash them thoroughly in running water. Cook them in a large pan with the water together with the onions and garlic until they open. Take from the pan with a slotted spoon. Strain the liquid through muslin or a fine sieve. Shell the mussels and put aside until required. Return the liquid to the pan and slowly bring to the boil. Combine the flour with enough milk to make a thin paste, stir this into the liquid, reheat and continue cooking gently for 10 minutes.

Add the mussels but cook them only just long enough to reheat or they will toughen. Sprinkle with pepper and chopped parsley and serve at once.

Vermicelli Soup

SHERIYELI ÇORBA (Turkey and Greece)

For 4–6

110g (¼lb/about 2 cups US) fine vermicelli
1½l (3 pints/3¾US) chicken stock
2 egg yolks
juice 1 lemon
salt and pepper

Break the vermicelli into small lengths. Bring the stock to the boil, add the vermicelli, stir well and cook it until tender, 1 to 2 minutes. Beat the egg yolks well; gradually add the lemon juice, salt, pepper and about 1 tablespoon of the hot stock, stirring all the time. Mix well and pour into the soup just before serving.

Yogurt Soup

ASH MAST VA KHIR (Iran)

For 6

½ cup (⅔ US) stoneless raisins
4 cups (5 US) yogurt
½ cup (⅔ US) single cream
1 hard-boiled egg, chopped
1 small cucumber, peeled and diced
6 ice cubes
salt and pepper to taste

Garnish
finely chopped parsley and dill, or mint

Soak the raisins in warm water until they are plump. Drain and pat dry. Pour the yogurt into a large bowl, add the remaining ingredients, except the garnish, and mix well. Chill in the refrigerator and serve garnished with herbs.

Yogurt and Spinach Soup

LABANEYA (Egypt)

For 6

1kg (2¼lb) spinach
3 tablespoons (3¾ US) oil
1 large onion, chopped
110g (4oz/½ cup US) long grain rice
1½l (3 pints/3¾ US) warm water
salt and pepper
2 cups (2½ US) natural yogurt
2–3 cloves garlic, crushed

Wash the spinach, drain well and tear the leaves into strips. Heat the oil in a large pan, add the onion and cook gently until it is soft and begins to change colour. Add the spinach, stir it well into the onion and continue to cook gently for 10 minutes. Add the rice, stir again, add the water, salt and pepper. Bring to the boil and boil for 12 minutes or until the rice is soft. Beat the yogurt with the crushed garlic, take the pan off the heat, add the yogurt to the soup and stir well. Return the pan to the heat and cook gently to just reheat – if the soup boils it will curdle.

An Iranian version of this soup, called Tribal Soup (*Ash Leban*), includes small cubes of mutton and crushed wheat. It is generally eaten in the spring when the sheep give an ample supply of milk to make a thick and rich yogurt.

Traditionally this soup is made with chard or beet, called *silq* in Egypt and *blette* in France.

Chicken and Yogurt Soup

TAVUK ÇORBASI YOĞURTLU (Turkey)

For 8–10

2l (3½ pints/4 US) chicken stock
60g (2oz/¼ cup US) long grain rice
salt and pepper to taste
1 tablespoon (1¼ US) flour
1 cup (1¼ US) yogurt
2 egg yolks, well beaten
2 cups (2½ US) warm water
30g (1oz/2 tablespoons US) butter or margarine
1 good tablespoon (1¼ US) finely chopped mint

Bring the stock to the boil, add the rice and cook it rapidly for 15 minutes. Add salt and pepper. While the rice is cooking, combine the flour, yogurt, egg yolks and water in another pan and cook slowly until almost boiling, stirring constantly. Add to the rice, stir well and simmer for 5 minutes. Melt the butter, add the mint, stir and pour this over the soup when in the bowls.

Courgette Soup

KOUSA (Lebanon)

For 6

½kg (about 1lb) courgettes or vegetable marrow
salt
30g (1oz/2 tablespoons US) butter
milk (see below)
2 tablespoons (2½ US) flour
black pepper and chopped parsley

Peel the courgettes, cut into chunks and cook in salted water until very soft. Drain thoroughly and mash to a purée. Measure and put aside, and for each cup of purée you will need one cup of milk. Bring the milk to the boil. Heat the butter in a pan, add the flour and stir to a roux. Gradually add the milk, stirring all the time until the mixture is thick. Add the purée and continue cooking until hot. Serve sprinkled with freshly ground black pepper and finely chopped parsley.

Onion Soup

ESHKANEH (Iran)

For 6

60g (2oz/4 tablespoons US) butter or other fat
½kg (about 1lb) onions, thinly sliced
2l (3½ pints/4 US) warm water
2 tablespoons (2½ US) flour
salt and pepper
1–2 tablespoons sugar
½ cup (⅔ US) lemon juice
2 eggs

Garnish
1 tablespoon (1¼ US) dried mint
about ¼ teaspoon each cinnamon and pepper

Melt the butter in a large pan, add the onions and cook them slowly until soft but not brown. Mix enough water with the flour to make a thin paste, pour this slowly into the onions, stirring all the time to ensure it does not become lumpy. Gradually add the remaining water, still stirring, bring to a slow boil, lower the heat, add salt and pepper and continue cooking for about 30 minutes. Combine the sugar and lemon juice, stir this into the soup and continue cooking for another 10 minutes. Beat the eggs well. Rub the dried mint between the palms of the hand until it powders and mix with the cinnamon and pepper. Immediately before serving, take the pan from the heat, add the garnish and the eggs to the soup, stir well, cover and leave for 2 minutes without heat.

Tomato and Onion Soup

MUNAZALET BANADORA (Syria)

For 8–10

30g (1oz/2 tablespoons US) butter or other fat
2 large onions, sliced
½kg (about 1lb) breast of mutton or lamb, cubed
1kg (2¼lb) firm tomatoes, peeled and chopped
3–4 cloves garlic, crushed
1 tablespoon (1¼ US) tomato concentrate
1½l (3 pints/3¾ US) warm water
salt to taste
½ teaspoon (US) pepper

Heat the fat in a large pan, add the onions and cook them until soft and just brown. Add the meat and garlic, stir well, cover the pan and simmer for 15 minutes. Cover with the tomatoes and continue simmering. Dilute the tomato concentrate with the warm water, add salt and pepper and pour this liquid over the top of the tomatoes. Cover and continue cooking very slowly for about 2 hours. When fresh tomatoes are not available, whole canned tomatoes may be substituted, but omit the tomato concentrate. Serve hot with boiled rice.

Lentil Soup

SHOURABAT ADAS (Syria and Lebanon)

For 6–8

225g (½lb/1 heaped cup US) lentils, previously soaked
60g (2oz/4 tablespoons US) clarified butter or other fat
1 large onion, coarsely chopped
salt to taste
½ cup (⅔ US) long grain rice (optional)
2 tablespoons (2½ US) lemon juice

Cook the lentils in about 1½l (3 pints/3¾ US) of water until soft. (Cooking time varies according to the type of lentils used.) Heat the fat and fry the onion until brown. When the lentils are soft, rub them through a coarse sieve, return to the pan, add the salt and fried onion and cook gently for 10 minutes. If the soup is too thick add a little hot water. If using rice, cook this separately and add it to the lentils just before serving. Add the lemon juice and stir well.

The Turks serve a similar soup with a dressing of melted butter and paprika pepper which is decorative and enhances its flavour. In some recipes, finely chopped spinach is added to the soup after the lentils are cooked.

Sweet Corn Soup

MISIR ÇORBASI (Turkey)

For 6

1–2 red or green sweet peppers
60g (2oz/4 tablespoons US) butter
1 large onion, sliced
2 large tomatoes, peeled and chopped
$1\frac{1}{2}$l (3 pints/$3\frac{3}{4}$ US) warm light stock
30g (1oz/$\frac{1}{4}$ cup US) flour
1 large can sweet corn kernels, not creamed
salt and pepper

Cut open the peppers, remove the cores and seeds and thinly slice the flesh. Heat the butter in a large pan, add the onion and fry it gently until soft but not brown. Add the tomatoes and peppers, stir, add the stock and bring to a slow boil. Mix the flour with enough water (or milk) to make a thin paste. Gradually pour this into the soup, still stirring, cook for 5 minutes, add the corn and seasoning and cook gently for 15 minutes.

Groundnut Soup

FUL SUDANI (Egypt)

For 6

A soup of Sudanese origin.

½kg (about 1lb) fresh shelled peanuts
4 cups (5 US) milk
4 cups (5 US) stock
salt and pepper
cream and butter (optional)

Roast the shelled nuts in a hot oven until the skins can be removed easily. Leave to cool before rubbing off the skins. Put the nuts through the finest blade of a mincer or in a blender. Turn into a mixing bowl and gradually add the milk, stirring all the time. Add the stock, salt and pepper, pour into a large pan and slowly bring to the boil. Cook for 10 minutes, stirring frequently. Add a little cream and butter just before serving.

Mutton Soup

CHERVAH (Arab Bedouin)

For 8–10

60g (2oz/4 tablespoons US) butter or other fat
½kg (about 1lb) onions, dried
½kg (about 1lb) breast of lamb, cubed
3l (5 pints/6¼ US) warm water
225g (½lb) tomatoes, blanched and peeled
salt and pepper
1 tablespoon (1¼ US) dried mint
110g (¼lb/½ cup US) rice

Heat the fat in a large pan and fry the onions until brown. Add the meat, tomatoes, water, salt, pepper and mint and simmer until the meat is very tender. Add the rice and cook until soft, about 15 minutes.

Vermicelli, broken into small pieces, may be used instead of rice.

Wedding Soup

DÜĞÜN ÇORBASI (Turkey)

For 6–8

3l (5 pints/6¼ US) mutton stock
60g (2oz/½ cup US) flour
3 egg yolks or 2 whole eggs
juice 1 lemon

Garnish
60g (2oz/4 tablespoons US) melted butter
1 tablespoon (1¼ US) mild paprika

This is a favourite Turkish soup served, as its name suggests, at weddings but also at important functions or at 'public rejoicings'.

Make the stock with lamb or mutton bones with some meat attached. When the stock is ready, strain and pull off as much meat as possible from the bones. Return the stock to the pan plus the small pieces of meat and bring to a gentle boil. Mix the flour with sufficient water to make a thin paste and stir this slowly into the stock and continue cooking for another 5 minutes. Beat the eggs in a bowl until frothy, gradually add the lemon juice, beat again and add 1 ladleful of the stock. Beat well, then pour this mixture into the soup, stirring all the time. Continue cooking over a very low heat for 2 minutes; if the heat is too high, the sauce will curdle. Melt the butter in a small pan, add the paprika, stir well and pour this over the soup after serving.

Almond Soup

BADEM ÇORBASI (Turkey)

For 6

225g (½lb) almonds, ground
6 hard-boiled egg yolks
6 bitter almonds, ground
1 teaspoon (1¼ US) coriander seeds
1 teaspoon (1¼ US) lemon rind
4 cups (5 US) warm chicken stock
2 cups (2½ US) single cream

Pound the ground almonds, egg yolks, bitter almonds, lemon rind and coriander seeds together in a mortar and mix with 1 ladleful of stock to a paste (or put it all in a blender). Put the rest of the stock in a large pan, bring to the boil, then stir in the almond paste. Cook gently for 10 minutes. Take the pan from the heat, add the cream, stirring all the while. Return the pan to the stove and, still stirring, continue cooking until the soup is reheated. Do not let it boil or the cream will curdle.

Avocado Pear Soup

MARAK AVOCADO (Israel)

For 4

2 large avocado pears
45g (1½oz/3 tablespoons US) butter
45g (1½oz/3 tablespoons US) flour
2 cups (2½ US) milk
2 cups (2½ US) warm chicken stock
salt and pepper
croûtons and paprika or sliced lemon as garnish

Cut the avocado pears into halves, remove stones, scoop out all the flesh and mash this until smooth. Put aside. Heat the butter in a saucepan, add the flour and stir to a roux. Gradually add the chicken stock, stirring all the time, then the milk, still stirring. Cook over a moderate heat until the mixture thickens, add salt and pepper, then cook slowly for 5 minutes. Add the mashed avocado, stir well and continue cooking for a further 2 minutes. Serve hot, garnished with *croûtons* and paprika or sliced lemon.

Cold Fruit Soup

MARAK PEIROTKARIM (Israel)

For 6

1kg (2¼lb) mixed fruits
about 110g (4oz/½ cup US) sugar
about 2½l (4½ pints/5¼ US) water
1 teaspoon (1¼ US) cinnamon
good pinch salt
15g (½oz/1 tablespoon US) cornflour
fresh or sour cream as a garnish

Israelis use apples, quinces, strawberries, apricots, peaches, raspberries, mulberries, grapes, persimmons, and mangoes to make fruit soups. The quantity of water and sugar varies with the type of fruit used. They are served chilled and usually garnished with fresh or sour cream.

Cook the fruit with the sugar, water, cinnamon and salt until soft. Strain, remove stones and rub the fruit through a sieve. Return to the pan. Mix the cornflour with a little warm water to a thin paste, stir this into the fruit and cook over a low heat for 10 minutes, stirring constantly. Cool and chill before serving with fresh or sour cream.

Walnut and Grape Juice Soup

ASH SACK (Iran)

For 6

1kg ($2\frac{1}{4}$lb) spinach
1 large onion, thinly sliced
1–2 leeks, cleaned and sliced
chopped parsley to taste
2l ($3\frac{1}{2}$ pints/4 US) warm water
2 tablespoons ($2\frac{1}{2}$ US) ground rice
3 eggs
225g ($\frac{1}{2}$lb) lamb or beef, minced
4–5 tablespoons unsweetened grape juice
110g (4oz/1 cup US) walnut meats, crushed

Wash and clean the spinach, drain, chop and put into a large pan with the onion, leeks, parsley and water. Bring to the boil. Mix the ground rice with sufficient water to make a thin paste. Stir this into the soup and continue cooking over a moderate heat until the vegetables are tender. Beat 1 egg and mix with the meat, kneading it well. Break off small pieces and shape into tiny balls. Drop these into the soup and continue cooking for 15 minutes. Beat the remaining eggs with the grape juice and pour this into the soup a few minutes before serving. Serve the walnuts separately as a garnish.

Fish

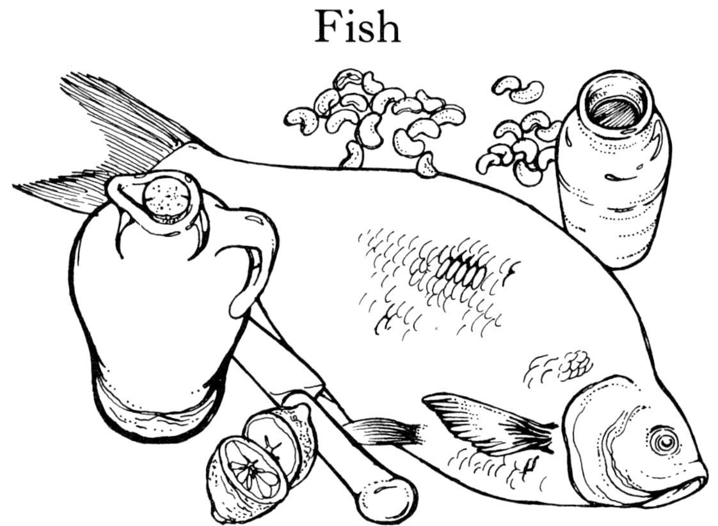

A tremendous variety of fish is found in Mediterranean waters and there can be no doubt of the incredible quantity of good edible fish, all worth sampling.

As far as the Turks are concerned, fish is important from the moment when it is taken from the nets, whisked quickly to the markets and displayed to show up all their subtle colours, like patterns in a kaleidoscope. The scarlet gills of the smaller fish are pulled out to look like a frill, while those of the larger fish are so stiffened they look like birds of paradise. Fish in Istanbul is sold literally out of the sea by fishermen from their painted boats tied up by Galata Bridge, where the Golden Horn and the Bosphorus meet. Here there is a free for all, all trying to beat down the fisherman's price, whose catch, he declares 'in the name of Allah' is the best.

The Greeks too are experts in the matter of dealing with

fish, serving baby clams and sea urchins straight from the sea, and cutting octopus and squid into tiny rings to fry until crisp, serving them amidst toasted nuts. The ancient Greeks, we are told, were the discoverers of oysters but, whatever the ancients may have felt about them, modern Greeks scorn them as dirty eaters. A favourite method of cooking fish is to grill over charcoal; almost as popular are fish stews and soups, many being a variation on a theme. The Greeks always serve wedges of lemon with fish.

In some parts of the Middle East fish is allied with superstition. In Iran, where there are not many recipes for its cooking, fish is served on New Year's Day to 'cleanse' the people and protect them from evil. In Israel, a whole fish is served on festive occasions, the head being given to the master of the house as a token of his wisdom and leadership. Most Israeli fish dishes are taken from every quarter of the world, with the carp predominating and cooked in every possible manner, and herring dishes coming a close second. Small fish are also popular, probably because, according to *The Talmud*, 'he who makes a habit of eating small fish does not suffer from indigestion', but, maybe more importantly, because 'small fish make a man's whole body fruitful and virile'.

In the Levant generally there is a lack of precision when talking of fish, and recipes tend to say 'take a fish' or maybe '2 kilos of white fish'. Syria has a much appreciated fish, the sollar, which is so hideous it is decapitated immediately it is caught. A favourite Lebanese fish is the Sultan Ibrahim which is usually fried and served hot with sauces, such as mayonnaise or *tahina*, as indeed are most of the Lebanese fish.

Curiously Iraq, despite the Tigris and the Euphrates, and its comparative closeness to the Persian Gulf, is not rich in fish dishes. Their most famous fish is the masgoof. Although the Iraqis claim they appreciate fish, the fact that so many of their dishes are heavily spiced and seasoned would suggest the fish are not as flavoursome as the Iraqis would like.

Finally, fish dishes are meant as a main course in the Middle Eastern region.

Fish with Rice

SAYYADIYYA (Lebanon and Middle East)

For 6–8

There are many versions of this popular Middle East recipe. The following is one of the more simple. In some Arab cookbooks this dish is included among the soups.

1 large white fish, about 1kg ($2\frac{1}{4}$lb)
2 cups ($2\frac{1}{2}$ US) long grain rice
1 cup ($1\frac{1}{4}$ US) olive oil
2–3 onions, finely sliced
salt and cumin to taste
juice 1 lemon

Clean the fish and leave in salted iced water for one hour. Drain, pat dry and cut into pieces. Put aside. Wash the rice and soak for 30 minutes and drain. Heat the oil in a large pan, add the onions and either fry them until soft and transparent, or until soft and a dark brown, thus making a brown *sayyadiyya*. Add 4 cups (5 US) of warm water and cook until the onions are almost dissolved. Rub through a coarse sieve. Return the onion liquid to the pan, add salt and cumin, then the fish and cook until tender but still firm, about 15 minutes. Take the fish from the pan and put aside – if the dish is to be served hot, keep it hot, otherwise it can remain warm, it is served either way. Take out some of the liquid from the pan, leaving about two cups ($2\frac{1}{2}$ US); put this liquid aside and bring that remaining in the pan to the boil. Dribble in the rice, let it boil for 2 minutes, then lower the heat, cover the pan and simmer for 15 minutes; turn off the heat and leave the rice for another 15 minutes. In the meantime, cook the remaining fish stock with the lemon juice, simmering until it has reduced by about a half.

Serve the rice heaped on a hot platter, garnished with the fish and the hot lemon sauce poured over the top. Or, if preferred, serve the rice and fish separately and the sauce in a sauceboat on the side.

Baked Fish

SAMAK MASCHWI
(Lebanon, but common to Middle East)

For 6

Mullet is preferred for this dish but other seafish can be baked in the same manner.

6 medium-sized mullet
salt
olive oil
6 pieces parchment or foil
coarsely chopped parsley
lemon juice
freshly ground black pepper

Clean the fish thoroughly, leaving the heads and tails intact. Wash well under running water, rub inside and out with salt and leave for an hour or so in the refrigerator. Bring the fish once again to room temperature and rub them generously with olive oil. Wrap each fish in paper, making sure the ends are tightly sealed, and place the packages on a baking sheet. Bake in a preheated hot oven (220C, 425F, Mark 7) for about 45 minutes. Combine the parsley and lemon juice with a little oil, salt and pepper.

Serve the fish still wrapped in its paper, with the parsley and lemon mixture separately, to be poured over the fish when the packages are opened.

An equally popular Lebanese version of this dish is one using a whole but large white fish. The eyes are removed and the head and tail left intact. It is prepared in the same manner as the mullet and baked until the fish is quite tender and the flesh white. For serving, it is taken from the paper and arranged on a serving platter garnished with stoned black and green olives, small sprigs of parsley and strips of sweet peppers. Bowls of mayonnaise or *tarator* (see page 65) and slices of lemon are served separately.

Fish Baked in a Vegetable Sauce

SAMAK YAKHNI (Egypt)

For 6–8

1kg ($2\frac{1}{4}$lb) white fish
juice 2–3 lemons
salt and pepper
1–2 teaspoons cumin seeds
$\frac{1}{2}$ cup ($\frac{2}{3}$ US) olive oil
$\frac{1}{2}$kg (about 1lb) onions, finely chopped
3–4 cloves garlic, crushed
small bunch parsley, finely chopped
handful celery leaves, finely chopped
2–3 bay leaves
225g ($\frac{1}{2}$lb) tomatoes, peeled and chopped

Cut the fish into 6 or 8 pieces. Mix the lemon juice, salt, pepper and cumin seeds, beat well then pour this mixture over the fish and leave in a cool place for an hour or so. Heat the oil, add the onions and garlic and gently fry until beginning to change colour. Add the parsley and celery, stir well, add the bay leaves and tomatoes, stir again and simmer for 20 to 30 minutes. This is called a *yakhni* or sauce. Pour half the sauce into a fireproof baking dish, add the fish then the rest of the sauce, spreading it well over the fish. Cover with foil or oiled paper and bake in a moderate oven (180C, 350F, Mark 4) until the fish is tender, about 30 minutes.

The fish can be served hot with rice, or cold with yogurt flavoured with chopped garlic, parsley or mint, salt and pepper. In Turkey, also the Lebanon, yogurt and fish are never served together as this is considered dangerous to the health.

Baked Fresh Sardines

PSARI RIYÀNATO (Greece)

For 4–6

1kg ($2\frac{1}{4}$lb) fresh sardines
6 tablespoons ($\frac{1}{2}$ cup US) olive oil
juice 2 lemons
salt
oregano (see page 18)

Clean the sardines and arrange in a shallow baking dish. Beat the oil with the lemon juice and pour this mixture over the fish. Add salt and oregano to taste and bake in a moderate, preheated oven (180C, 350F, Mark 4) until tender, 25 to 30 minutes.

Serve as a main dish or as a starter.

Baked Fish in a Wine Sauce

PSARI FOURNOU ME KRASSI (Greece)

For 4–6

1 large white fish
salt and pepper
olive oil
2 cups ($2\frac{1}{2}$ US) tepid water
2 cups ($2\frac{1}{2}$ US) dry white wine
2 teaspoons ($2\frac{1}{2}$ US) dry mustard

Make a slit in the belly of the fish large enough to clean inside. Do not remove head and tail. Rub inside and out with salt and pepper and place in a generously oiled baking pan. Mix the water, wine and mustard and add to the pan. Bake in a moderate oven (180C, 350F, Mark 4) until the fish is tender, basting from time to time. If the sauce should reduce too much before the fish is tender and flaky at the touch of a fork, add more wine. Allow 10 minutes baking for each $\frac{1}{2}$kg (about 1lb) of fish. If the fish is lean, gash the skin in two or three places before cooking to keep it from bursting.

Fish Baked in Onion Sauce

PSARI ME SALTSA KREMITHIA (Greece)

For 6

2–3 large onions
salt to taste
1 tablespoon (1¼ US) lemon juice
3 large tomatoes, peeled and sliced
1 large fish, about 1¼kg (3lb)
finely chopped parsley to taste
pepper to taste
capers to taste (optional)
olive oil

Peel and thickly slice the onions and cook in boiling, salted water with the lemon juice until soft. Clean the fish and cut into thick slices; remove any awkward bones without actually filleting it. Add the fish to the pan on top of the onions and cook over a moderate heat for 10 minutes. Spread a baking dish with tomatoes, add the fish pieces, parsley, pepper, capers and several tablespoonfuls of olive oil. Strain the onions and spread these over the top, then add enough of the onion liquid to almost cover and bake in a preheated moderate oven (180C, 350F, Mark 4) until the fish is tender and flaky.

Baked Fish with Tahina and Walnuts

SAMAK BIL RASHI (Middle East)

For 6

6 firm white fish steaks, filleted
1 cup (1¼ US) lemon juice
salt
½ cup (⅔ US) olive oil
3 large onions, sliced
1 cup (1¼ US) blanched walnuts
½ cup (⅔ US) tahina (see page 20)
parsley for garnishing

Wash the fish, pat dry, rub well with some of the lemon juice, sprinkle with salt and leave for 2 to 3 hours in a refrigerator. Heat the oil, fry the fish on both sides until just brown, then place in a flat, well-oiled baking dish. In the same oil fry the onions until they are soft and begin to change colour. Spread the onions over the top of the fish. Crush or coarsely grind the walnuts and sprinkle these over the top. Mix the *tahina* with the remaining lemon juice, beat until creamy, then add just enough tepid water to make a thin paste. Pour this over the top of the walnuts. Bake in a preheated moderate oven (180C, 350F, Mark 4) until the fish is tender, about 20 minutes. Leave until cold, but do not refrigerate, and serve garnished with parsley.

Fish Cooked in a Cumin Sauce

KAMMOUNIĀL SAMAK (Egypt)

For 4

¼ head garlic
1 teaspoon (1¼ US) ground cumin
3–4 tablespoons oil
2 cups (2½ US) tomato juice
about ½ cup water
salt and pepper
½kg (about 1lb) white fish

Peel and crush the garlic and mix with the cumin. Heat the oil in a saucepan, add the garlic and cook for 5 to 7 minutes. Add the tomato juice and cook for 5 minutes; add the water, salt and pepper and bring to the boil. Add the fish, cover the pan and cook over a low heat for 15 to 20 minutes, or until the fish is flaky. Serve with rice.

Fried Fish

SAMAK MAQLI (Lebanon)

Any white fish can be used in this recipe but for frying the Lebanese prefer the fish they call Sultan Ibrahim, serving one or two per person with a sauce.

fish
salt
olive oil
flour

Clean and scale the fish, remove the eyes but leave the heads and tails intact. Sprinkle inside and out with salt and leave in the refrigerator for several hours. Before frying, return them to room temperature. Heat the oil; you need a good half-an-inch of oil in the pan. Lightly coat the fish in flour and fry until lightly browned, shaking the pan from time to time to prevent sticking, and turn each fish once. Serve hot with a sauce, such as mayonnaise, *tarator bi tahina* (see page 66), or a mixture of crushed pine-nuts mixed with lemon juice, crushed garlic and salt. Garnish with spring onions, small radishes and wedges of lemon.

In the Lebanon small pieces of Arab bread are fried in the fish oil and also served as a garnish.

Grilled Swordfish Steaks

KILIÇ BALIĞI IZGARASI (Turkey)

For 6

1kg (2¼lb) swordfish
juice 1 lemon
1 good tablespoon (1¼ US) olive oil
1 tablespoon (1¼ US) onion juice (see note)
cayenne pepper to taste
salt to taste

Dressing
juice 1 lemon
2 tablespoons (2½ US) olive oil
1 tablespoon (1¼ US) finely chopped parsley

Pull off its thick skin and cut the fish into thick steaks. Put into a dish. Combine the next five ingredients and pour this as a marinade over the fish. Leave for 5 hours or so.

Prepare the dressing by combining the rest of the ingredients and beat the mixture well.

Grill the steaks. Obviously the best way is over charcoal but, failing this, by whatever means at your disposal.

Serve the fish hot with the dressing.

Note : To make 1 tablespoon of onion juice, mince 1 small onion and squeeze it through a piece of muslin.

Fish Kebabs

SAMAK KEBAB (Egypt)

For 6

675g ($1\frac{1}{2}$lb) firm white fish, filleted
juice 2–3 lemons
juice 2–3 onions
3 bay leaves
1–2 teaspoons cumin, powdered
salt and pepper to taste
6–8 small firm tomatoes
olive oil
coarsely chopped parsley

Cut the fish into cubes about 2cm ($\frac{3}{4}$in) thick. Mix the lemon and onion juices, bay leaves, cumin, salt and pepper and pour this mixture over the fish, turning the pieces to make sure that each piece is well coated with the marinade. Leave aside for about an hour, longer if liked. Without peeling, cut the tomatoes into quarters or halves, depending on their size. Starting and finishing with a wedge of tomato, impale the pieces of fish and tomato alternately on to skewers. Brush lightly with olive oil (do this with a small brush or feather) and grill over charcoal. Serve on a bed of parsley, or watercress, with wedges of lemon, and an aubergine purée (see page 25).

St Peter's Fish-Grilled

DAG-YAM-KINNERET BE'GRILL (Israel)

For 6

St Peter's fish, a variety of trout, lives in the Sea of Galilee, a descendant of the fish St Peter harvested in such quantities. It is a silver and blue fish which can weigh up to 1kg ($2\frac{1}{4}$lb) and measure about 30cm (1ft) in length at maturity. It is still grilled over wood embers or charcoal in Israel, in much the same manner as in the days of St Peter.

6 small trout
oil
salt, pepper and sprigs parsley
6 slices onion
juice 1 lemon

Rub the grill with oil. Brush the fish inside and out with oil, salt, freshly ground pepper and put a sprig of parsley and a slice of onion into each fish. Grill the fish, two or three at a time depending on the size of the grill, until the skin is crisp and brown, then turn and brown the other side. As the fish cooks, brush it often with a mixture of oil and lemon juice. Each fish takes roughly 7 minutes to cook on either side. Serve immediately, garnished with wedges of lemon.

Grilled Fish with Oregano

PSARI ME RIYANI (Greece)

Since antiquity grilling fish over hot charcoal has been a speciality of fish cooking in Greece, a method which brings out its fullest flavour.

fish, whole or in portions
salt and pepper
olive oil
lemon juice
oregano (see page 18)

If possible choose red mullet or daurade for this dish to achieve the authentic flavour.

Clean the fish, rub it well with salt and pepper, brush with oil and sprinkle with lemon juice and finely chopped oregano. If using whole fish, do not cut off the head and tail. Failing a charcoal grill, the fish can be grilled by whatever means at your disposal but basted frequently with lemon juice and brushed with olive oil. When one side of the fish is browned, turn it and repeat this process until it is cooked through. If the fish is large and whole, turn it twice. If smaller fish or cutlets are used, these need turning once only. Serve the fish straight from the grill, sprinkled with freshly chopped oregano and garnished with wedges of lemon.

In Greece, for local taste, the fish is served with a bitter salad, such as spinach mixed with rocket.

Soused Anchovies

HAMSI BUĞULAMSI (Turkey)

For 6

1kg ($2\frac{1}{4}$lb) fresh anchovies
6 tablespoons ($\frac{1}{2}$ cup US) olive oil
1 cup ($1\frac{1}{4}$ US) water
salt
2 tablespoons ($2\frac{1}{2}$ US) finely chopped dill
2 tablespoons ($2\frac{1}{2}$ US) finely chopped parsley
juice 1 lemon

Clean, wash and pat the anchovies dry, leaving their heads and tails intact. Place them side by side in a fish frying-pan, add the oil, water, salt – not too much, dill and parsley. Cover the pan and cook for 8 to 10 minutes over a moderate heat. Take the pan from the heat, sprinkle the fish with lemon juice and leave until cold. Serve with their sauce.

Red mullet, fresh sardines and other small fish are cooked in the same manner. Serve as a main dish or as a starter.

Cold Mackerel (Mackerel Stew Sultan's Style)

USKUMRU PAPAZ YAHNISI (Turkey)

For 3–6

3 large or 6 small mackerel
$\frac{1}{2}$ cup ($\frac{2}{3}$ US) olive oil
4 medium-sized onions, chopped
2 carrots, thinly sliced
4–6 cloves garlic, chopped
1 tablespoon ($1\frac{1}{4}$ US) tomato concentrate
2 cups ($2\frac{1}{2}$ US) warm water
salt and pepper to taste

Wash, clean and scale the mackerel, cut off the heads and tails, wipe dry and make two or three incisions in each fish. Put the olive oil into a pan, add the onions and cook gently until they are soft. Add the carrots and garlic and continue cooking until the onions are browned. Mix the tomato concentrate with the water, add to the pan, stir well and continue to cook over a moderate heat for 15 minutes. Place the fish side by side on top of the onions, sprinkle with salt and pepper and continue cooking until the mackerel are tender, about 15 minutes. Cool the fish in their sauce and serve cold from the pan with wedges of lemon and soft brown bread.

Boiled Carp

CARPION ME'VUSHAL (Israel)

For 6

Carp has long been a favourite fish with the Jewish people and freshwater fish still remains an important item in the diet of the Israelis. Natural looking ponds for breeding carp have been constructed throughout Israel, altering and enhancing the landscape in many areas. So important is the freshness of the carp that it is brought home alive from the fishmonger and left in a bucket until killed, or the housewife asks the fishmonger to kill it while she waits, then rushes home to cook it immediately.

1¼kg (3lb) fresh carp
coarse salt
½kg (about 1lb) onions, finely sliced
freshly ground pepper
2–3 lumps sugar
12 almonds, blanched and shredded
20 large seedless raisins

Scale, clean and wash the carp and rub inside and out with coarse salt. Leave for 30 minutes then rinse the fish in cold running water and cut into 6 slices. Put the onions at the bottom of a pan (preferably a fish kettle) and lay the fish on top, including the head and tail. Sprinkle with salt and pepper, add the sugar, almonds and raisins. Just cover with water, cover the pan and simmer until the fish flakes easily with a fork, about 1½ hours.

Remove the fish to a platter and reconstruct it to its original shape on a heated oval serving dish. Strain the stock and spread the cooked onions, by now a purée, over the top of the fish. Chill the stock in the refrigerator until almost jelled, then pour it over the fish and leave until it has quite jelled.

Fish Stew

KACCAVIA or CACCAVIA (Greece)

For 4–6

According to the Greeks, their cooks originated *bouillabaisse* which is the relic of an ancient fish soup called *kaccavia* introduced by the Greeks to the Marseilla Phocaem Colonies. The name is derived from the name of an earthenware pot, *kaccavia*, in which the fishermen used to cook soup in their fishing boats around which they would sit and help themselves. The French name also is derived from the pot in which the French cook their fish soup, *bouillote*. There is no 'one' recipe for this dish of fish, which has been described as 'the survival of something ancient'.

1–1½kg (about 2–3lb) mixed fish
onions to taste, sliced
tomatoes, peeled and chopped
1 cup (1¼ US) olive oil
salt and pepper

Cut the fish into serving pieces, using as many varieties as available, including if possible lobster, prawns and shrimps. Put enough water into a pan to poach the fish, add plenty of onions, tomatoes and the olive oil (this quantity can be halved if it seems too rich). Bring the liquid to the boil, add salt and pepper and continue to cook for 15 minutes by which time the water will look clear. Add the fish, the tougher variety first, for not all of them take the same time to cook. Cook the fish with the pot uncovered for 15 to 20 minutes. Serve the fish in its liquid.

Fish with Bananas

DAG IM BANAVOT (Israel)

For 4

flour, salt and pepper
4 large plaice fillets
110g (4oz/½ cup US) unsalted butter
2 bananas, ripe but firm
½–¾ cup almonds, slivered
juice ½ large lemon
2–3 tablespoons finely chopped parsley

Mix enough plain flour with salt and pepper to coat the fish. Heat half the butter and fry the fish on both sides until lightly browned, more golden than brown. Take from the pan. Add the rest of the butter and gently heat. Peel and halve the bananas lengthwise and lightly fry until golden. Arrange half a banana on each fillet of fish. Quickly fry the almonds in the remaining butter in the pan, stirring all the while as they quickly brown and burn. Take the pan from the heat, add the lemon juice and parsley, swirl these ingredients together (including the almonds) and pour this sauce over the fish.

Fish in an Orange Sauce

DAG B'MITZ TAPUZIM (Israel)

For 6

1kg (2¼lb) firm white fish fillets
flour
olive oil
1 cup (1¼ US) fresh orange juice
salt to taste
15g (½oz/1 tablespoon US) cornflour
1 small orange

Serve hot or cold. Wash and wipe dry the fish. Lightly coat with flour. Heat the oil, fry the fish on both sides until just brown, put into a serving dish and leave to cool if serving cold; put into a warm oven if serving hot. Make the sauce. Bring the orange juice to the boil, add salt. Make a thin paste with the cornflour and water, stir this into the orange juice and cook over a low heat, stirring all the while, until the sauce thickens. Pour this over the fish. If serving cold, allow the fish to become cold in its sauce – but do not refrigerate.

Serve garnished with peeled orange segments and with boiled potatoes, peas, or a vegetable *macédoine* separately.

Squid Cooked in Wine

KALAMARIA KATHISTA (Cyprus)

For 4–6

½kg (about 1lb) cleaned squid or inkfish
½ cup (⅔ US) oil
3 large onions, sliced
small piece cinnamon stick
4 cloves garlic, crushed
salt to taste
1–2 bay leaves
½ cup (⅔ US) red or white wine, dry
½ cup (⅔ US) vinegar

Cut the squid into rings. Heat the oil, add the onions and fry for a minute or so, then add the fish and fry until the onions are soft. Add the remaining ingredients, cover the pan and cook over a low heat for about 1 hour or until the fish is tender and all the liquid has been absorbed. Discard the bay leaves and cinnamon and serve with boiled rice.

Fried Salt Cod Fritters with Garlic Sauce

BAKALIAROS SKORTHALIA (Greece)

For 4–6

½kg (about 1lb) salt cod
skorthalia sauce (see page 65)
olive oil for deep frying

Batter
110g (¼lb) flour
salt
1 tablespoon (1¼ US) olive oil
½ cup (⅔ US) tepid water
white 1 large egg

Salt cod looks like strips of old wood and requires considerable soaking when bought absolutely dry. Soak between 24 and 36 hours in six to eight changes of cold water until it looks white and is almost flaky. Remove skin and bones, drain, pat the fish dry and cut into 5cm (2in) pieces.

Make the skorthalia sauce. Then make the batter: mix the flour with a pinch of salt, add the oil, mix well, then add the water, beating the mixture thoroughly. Beat the egg white until stiff and fold it carefully into the batter.

Heat plenty of olive oil, dip the pieces of fish into the batter and fry a few pieces at a time until brown. Take out, drain and keep warm while the rest of the fritters are being fried. Serve hot with the sauce.

A plate of radishes often accompanies this dish. In the Mediterranean salt cod can be bought pre-soaked as well as absolutely dried.

Vegetables

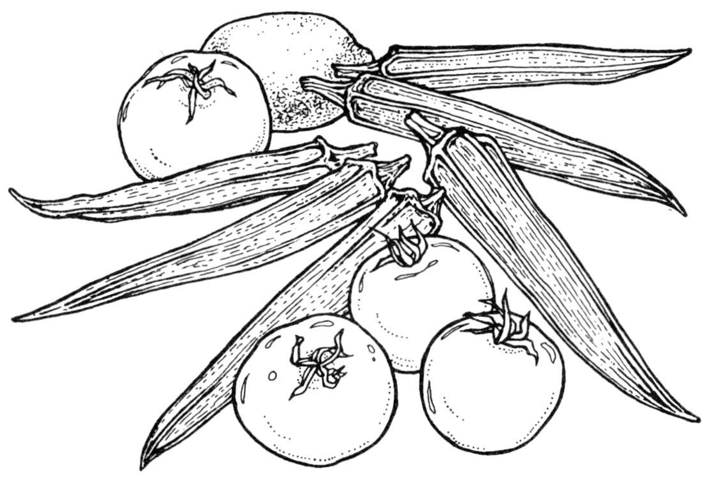

There should be little difficulty nowadays in obtaining anywhere the vegetables required for Middle Eastern cooking. Even the British, considered conservative in their cooking and choice of vegetables, no longer regard aubergines and sweet peppers as exotic vegetables; these are now found in shops and markets throughout the country, also in the seed catalogues. It is of interest to note that this exchange of vegetables is not entirely one way. About 100 years ago an Englishman, Sir John Malcolm, introduced potatoes into Iran (where they have not taken on well) and for a long time they were known as 'Malcolm's plums'.

Vegetables hold an important place in the cooking of the Middle East and are rarely cooked simply or even alone, but with rice, meat and fish, when they are combined to make substantial dishes for a main course.

Although the vegetables called for in this chapter are now familiar to almost everyone, perhaps a little advice will not come amiss. For example, aubergines, among the great vegetables of the world, also called eggplant, egg apple and garden apple, grow in abundance wherever the sun shines, and come in different shapes, sizes and colours. Those which are long and fat are the best for stuffing; the pear-shaped and round ones are for stewing, or turning into 'caviar' (see page 25). These types usually are purple to blue-black in colour. There also is a small, ivory-white, egg-shaped aubergine which grows in America (and elsewhere) from which the Americans gave all aubergines the name of eggplant.

Artichokes are popular, particularly in Greece and Turkey, but not so easily obtained outside of their normal habitats. However, canned and frozen artichokes can be used in many of the ways in which fresh artichokes are used. Cucumbers in the Middle East are worthy of special mention. Small and sturdy in appearance, it is not for nothing that they are described as 'small and sweet as a baby's fingers'. Served cut into 'sticks', they are incredibly juicy, lacking in the acidity which causes embarrassing digestive problems. In Iran they grow a delicately flavoured cucumber which is served as a fruit. Swiss chard and spinach are both important in this area. Local spinach, both tender and flavoursome, is a dark, almost curly-leafed variety which grows in a bunch from one small root.

Okra, called ladies' fingers in Britain, is probably one of the least known vegetables from the Middle East, also one not to everyone's taste. It can be rather glutinous, therefore, it is important not to cut into the green pod itself when taking off the stalk. Kept whole and properly cooked, they can be most interesting. They are often sold fresh in Greek and Indian shops, also canned. Although the USA cans and exports okra, the pods are cut in a manner which does not go well with Middle Eastern cooking.

Onions have been used in this region's cooking, especially in Egypt, for thousands of years. Generally the white onion is preferred but, obviously, other types can be substituted when these are not available.

An interesting vegetable is celeriac, also called celery root or turnip rooted celery, and is a variety of celery grown for its roots. It can be thinly pared and used raw in salads, and of course cooked, when it should be first thinly peeled. Capsicums, or sweet peppers or paprika peppers, need nowadays hardly any introduction. They vary in size from so-called small bird-peppers to the monstrous, and their colours from red, green, yellow and even a curious mottled mixture of all colours. It is often said that red peppers are less hot than other varieties, but this is not so and, indeed, it is the seeds of sweet peppers which are hot, not the flesh. Before being used, either raw or cooked, the core and seeds of *all* peppers must be removed for these certainly are hot. When choosing peppers, try to mix the colours, the flavours do not vary but the appearance of the dish is enhanced.

If capsicums need no introduction, do courgettes? These are grown in gardens and allotments everywhere. For stuffing, choose those of medium length and thickness; for slicing and frying, the larger ones are best, and the baby, tender courgettes can be cooked whole, or sliced thinly and used to make fritters or omelettes.

Finally, tomatoes, which have had many names before becoming the success story they are today. The tomatoes of the Middle East are usually sweet and often most curiously shaped. Today tomatoes are available fresh the year round, but for some dishes I prefer to use the strongly flavoured canned tomatoes from the Mediterranean region than the perfect-looking but often flavourless tomatoes of the winter months. For many recipes tomatoes must be peeled. This is simple. Plunge them into boiling water and leave for a minute or so, and the skins will peel off easily.

Ladies' Fingers with Tomatoes

BAMIA (Iraq and Turkey)

For 6

1kg ($2\frac{1}{4}$lb) ladies' fingers
oil for frying
225g ($\frac{1}{2}$lb) lamb, chopped
salt and pepper
a little lemon juice
$\frac{1}{2}$kg (about 1lb) tomatoes

Wash the ladies' fingers and dry thoroughly. Cut off the hard stem, taking care not to slash into the actual pods as this releases their glutinous content. Heat the oil and lightly fry the ladies' fingers – if over-fried, they will lose their colour. Arrange them round the sides of a shallow casserole (preferably one which can be brought to the table), leaving a well in the centre. This is best done by placing them pointed ends inwards and outwards alternately. The next layer is arranged in the same fashion but contrariwise, so that they are neatly inter-twined. Continue in this way until all the ladies' fingers are finished. Fill the centre with the chopped meat, or, as in Turkey, with a whole onion, sprinkle with salt, pepper and lemon juice and put aside.

Cook the tomatoes without adding any water until soft, rub through a sieve and pour the juice over the top of the ladies' fingers and meat. Cover the pan tightly and simmer until tender, about 40 minutes. Serve with rice.

Canned ladies' fingers can be used in a similar manner but first the meat must be half cooked, as canned ladies' fingers do not take so long to cook. When using canned ladies' fingers, place them in the pan without any particular arrangement for they are rather too soft to make any pattern, add the half-cooked meat, cover with the tomato juice and cook for 15 to 20 minutes. The point of serving ladies' fingers in a stove-to-table pan is that one should show off their intricate pattern. In Turkey they place a plate on top of the pan and swiftly turn the pan over, thus turning them out in a ring. I do not advise this unless you are a juggler.

Potato Rissoles

PATATES KÖFTESI (Turkey)

Makes 20–24 rissoles

1kg (2¼lb) potatoes
110g (¼lb) sharp-flavoured cheese, grated
30g (1oz/¼ cup US) flour
salt and pepper
1 egg, well beaten
oil for frying

Scrub the potatoes and cook them in salted water until soft. Peel as soon as possible and mash until smooth. Combine with the cheese, add the flour, salt, pepper and egg. Work this mixture to a firm dough and break off small pieces with floured hands. Shape these into 'sausages' and fry at once in deep hot oil to brown quickly. Serve hot or cold.

The mashed potatoes may also be flavoured with finely chopped parsley and grated onion, and less cheese used.

Spinach Pie

SPANAKOPITTA (Cyprus)

For 6

This recipe is one of many for spinach pie.

1kg (2¼lb) spinach
1 onion, finely chopped
finely chopped parsley to taste
salt and pepper
1 cup (1¼ US) béchamel sauce (see page 64)
60g (2oz/⅔ cup US) grated cheese
3 hard-boiled eggs, coarsely chopped
340g (¾lb) flaky pastry

Thoroughly wash the spinach in several waters, drain, chop and put into a pan without water. Add the onion, parsley, salt and pepper and cook until tender. Drain well and squeeze dry.

Make the béchamel sauce. Mix the cheese and eggs. Combine the béchamel, cheese and eggs with the spinach and mix well. Put aside.

Cut the pastry into half and roll out into two equal rounds. Grease a 25cm (10in) round baking tin and line it with one sheet of pastry. Spread with the spinach mixture, cover with the remaining pastry, press down round the edges, prick the top with a fork and cook in a preheated hot oven (220C, 425F, Mark 7) until the pie is a golden brown. Take from the oven and let the pie cool before cutting it.

This pie can be served as a starter or as a main dish with fried potatoes; it is at its best when cold, but not chilled.

The Dervish's Rosary – Baked Vegetable Casserole with Meat

MASBAHT EL DARWEESH (Lebanon)

For 6

2–3 tablespoons cooking fat
4 medium-sized onions, peeled and chopped
½kg (about 1lb) meat, minced
flour
½kg (about 1lb) potatoes, peeled and chopped
1–2 aubergines, peeled and chopped
4 medium-sized tomatoes, peeled and chopped
2–3 courgettes, peeled and sliced
water
salt and pepper to taste

Heat the fat in a fireproof oven casserole on top of the stove and fry the onions until they change colour. Add the meat, crumble it and fry until it begins to brown, sprinkle with flour, stir well, then add the remaining vegetables in the order given. Add water to cover, salt and pepper and bake in a preheated moderate oven (180C, 350F, Mark 4) until the vegetables are tender and the liquid has been absorbed. Stir from time to time. If the vegetables are cooked before the liquid has been absorbed, put the pan on top of the stove and cook uncovered over a moderate heat until it is absorbed. Serve hot.

French Beans with Meat

YAKNIT LOUBIEH (Middle East)

For 6–8

3 tablespoons (3¾ US) olive oil
2–3 onions, sliced
225g (½lb) meat, coarsely chopped
3 cups (3¾ US) stock or water
2–3 tomatoes, peeled and sliced, or 1 cup (1¼ US) tomato juice
1kg (2¼lb) French beans, trimmed but left whole
salt and pepper

Heat the oil in a saucepan and fry the onions until they begin to change colour. Add the meat (lamb or mutton is the usual choice) and fry until it is brown, shaking the pan from time to time to avoid sticking. Add the liquid, bring to the boil, add the tomatoes, beans, salt and pepper, cover the pan tightly and cook slowly for about 1 hour. Serve hot as a main dish.

Green Beans with Tomato and Onion

FASSOLAKIA FRESKA (Greece)

For 6–8

1kg (2¼lb) green beans
2–3 tablespoons oil
1–2 onions, sliced
1 tablespoon (1¼ US) tomato concentrate
salt and pepper to taste

Trim the beans and break into 2 or 3 pieces. Heat the oil in a saucepan, add the onion(s) and fry gently until they begin to change colour. Add the tomato concentrate and enough boiling water to just cover the beans, stir and bring to the boil. Add the beans, lower the heat, cover the pan and cook slowly for 30 to 45 minutes. Add salt and pepper just before serving. A main dish.

Artichokes in Oil

ENGINAR ZEYTINYAĞLI (Turkey)

For 6–8

6–8 large artichokes
15 spring onions or equivalent in mild onions, sliced
1–2 carrots, thinly sliced
½ cup (⅔ US) olive oil
juice 1 lemon
salt and pepper
1 scant tablespoon (1 US) sugar

Cook the artichokes in unsalted water until sufficiently tender to remove the leaves and the choke, about 20 minutes depending on age and freshness. Pull off the leaves, carefully leaving the heart as meaty as possible, and leave about 8cm (3in) of the stalk. As each artichoke is prepared put it back immediately into the stock to preserve its colour. When all are ready, put them into another pan, arranging them with the stalks uppermost, surround with the onions and carrots, add the oil, about 1 cup of water, the lemon juice, salt, pepper and sugar. Cover the pan tightly and cook over a low heat for about 1 hour, by which time most of the liquid will have evaporated and the artichokes will be tender. Cool and serve in any remaining sauce, plus the vegetables and slices of lemon.

Turkish artichokes are enormous yet full of flavour. It never ceased to give me childish pleasure to see the artichoke sellers with their paniers of enormous artichokes patrolling the streets yelling '*enginar*'. When fresh artichokes of such dimensions are not available, use canned ones. If preparing this dish with smaller artichokes, cook them for somewhat less time.

Artichoke Hearts and Broad Beans

ANGINARES ME KOYKIA (Greek-Turkish)

For 6

1kg (2¼lb) fresh broad beans
3–4 tablespoons olive oil
1 tablespoon (1¼ US) flour
juice 1 large lemon
finely chopped parsley to taste
salt and pepper
6 large canned artichoke hearts

Cook the beans in salted water until tender but firm. Drain, shell, put aside but keep warm; retain the liquid. Heat the oil in a saucepan, add the flour, stir to a roux, then gradually add enough liquid from the beans to make a thinnish sauce. Add the lemon juice, parsley and, if required, salt and pepper. Stir gently, add the artichokes and beans and simmer until the artichokes are hot. Cool and serve in the sauce with the beans.

If using fresh artichokes, prepare as in previous recipe but without the carrots and onions.

Stewed Leeks

PRATSA PILAKI (Cyprus)

For 4–6

1kg (2¼lb) leeks
2–3 carrots
4 tablespoons (5 US) olive oil
1 cup (1¼ US) warm water
salt and black pepper
1 tablespoon (1¼ US) long grain rice
2–3 firm tomatoes, peeled and quartered

Wash the leeks in running water to remove any grit or dirt between the leaves and discard any tough or broken outer leaves. Cut them into 5cm (2in) lengths. Scrape the carrots and slice into thin rings. Heat the oil in a saucepan, add the leeks and carrots, turn them until well covered with oil, add the water, salt and pepper, bring to the boil then add the rice.

Cover the pan and cook gently for 15 minutes, add the tomatoes and continue cooking until the leeks are tender. Usually served cold.

Leeks Sweet-Sour

PRASAH (Israel)

For 4–6

1kg ($2\frac{1}{4}$lb) leeks
4–5 tablespoons cooking oil
2 cloves garlic, crushed
1 tablespoon ($1\frac{1}{4}$ US) brown sugar
juice 2 lemons

Thoroughly wash the leeks and discard the tough or bruised outer leaves. Cut the leeks into lengths or thick rounds. Heat the oil, add the garlic and sugar and, stirring all the time, cook the sugar until it starts to become syrupy. Add the leeks, stir them well into the oil and cook until they begin to brown. Add the lemon juice, cover the pan and cook very slowly until the leeks are tender – cooking time depends on the age of the leeks. Serve hot or cold, with a main meat dish, or as a starter.

Stewed Pumpkin

KISHUYIM MEVUSHALIM (Israel)

For 6

30g (1oz/2 tablespoons US) butter
1 small onion, minced
1 large clove garlic, crushed
1 cup ($1\frac{1}{4}$ US) tomato juice
1kg ($2\frac{1}{4}$lb) pumpkin
juice 1 small lemon
salt and pepper to taste

Melt the butter in a large pan, add the onion and fry it gently until soft. Add the remaining ingredients, cover and cook over a simmering heat until the pumpkin is soft but not mushy, about 30 to 40 minutes according to the type and age of the pumpkin.

Boiled Potatoes

PATATES YAHNISI (Turkey)

For 4

1kg (2¼lb) potatoes
30g (1oz/2 tablespoons US) butter or margarine
1 tablespoon (1¼ US) flour
salt and pepper
chopped parsley to taste
2 bay leaves
1–2 tablespoons tomato concentrate
stock or water

Wash, peel and quarter the potatoes. Heat the butter in a large pan, add the flour and stir to a roux. Add salt, pepper, parsley and bay leaves, stir well, then add the tomato concentrate diluted in a little water; stir well, add the potatoes, stir again, add the stock to cover and cook gently, covered, until the potatoes are soft. Serve as a main dish.

This dish is even better if made with small, whole new potatoes, scrubbed but not scraped.

Aubergines with Onions and Tomatoes

MELITZANES YAHNI (Greece and Levant)

For 6

2–3 aubergines
salt
about 1½ cups (1⅞ US) olive oil
1 large onion, sliced
plenty chopped parsley
3–4 tomatoes, peeled and sliced
garlic to taste, slivered

Peel and slice the aubergines, sprinkle with salt and put between two large plates, heavily weighted. Leave for 1 hour, then rinse free of salt and wipe dry. Heat the oil in a deep pan, add the aubergine slices and fry until lightly brown on both sides. Lift from the pan and put aside. Add the onion to the pan, fry until brown, then return the aubergine slices. Add the remaining ingredients and continue to cook for about 45 minutes. Can be served hot or cold.

This type of dish is popular throughout the area and is similar to the Provençale dish *ratatouille*. It is difficult to give exact quantities of oil for cooking aubergines as they absorb a great deal. In the Levant the oil would remain in the dish for serving, but if this seems to be rather too much, pour off what seems to be excess.

Cauliflower Ragoût

MISSATRAAT QARNABIT or QARNABIT (Egypt)

For 6

1¼kg (3lb) cauliflower
1 cup (1¼ US) oil
1 large onion, minced
½kg (about 1lb) minced meat
4–6 tomatoes, peeled and thickly sliced
salt and pepper
1 cup (1¼ US) stock or water

Wash the cauliflower, break into flowerets and cook in lightly salted water until almost tender. Drain. Heat the oil, add the cauliflower and fry until golden brown. Take from the oil with a slotted spoon and put aside. In the same oil fry the onion until it changes colour, then add the meat and fry until it browns, stirring from time to time. Add the tomatoes and seasoning and cook until a thick sauce is formed. Spread the meat and tomato sauce on the bottom of a large casserole, cover neatly with the cauliflower, then add the stock. Cook in a moderate oven (180C, 350F, Mark 4) until the cauliflower is tender, about 45 minutes. Serve hot as a main dish.

Baked Aubergine

MOUSAKA (The Levant)

For 6–8

There are many variations of *mousaka*, a name which does not only imply aubergines but many kinds of baked or steamed vegetables. For example, there are cauliflower and potato *mousakas*.

3 good-sized aubergines
salt and pepper
3 egg yolks
2 cups ($2\frac{1}{2}$ US) milk
oil for deep frying
2–3 large onions, sliced
2–3 cloves garlic, slivered
$\frac{1}{2}$kg (about 1lb) cooked minced meat
3–4 tablespoons tomato concentrate
1 cup ($1\frac{1}{4}$ US) meat stock

Peel and slice the aubergines. Sprinkle with salt and leave for 2 hours between two heavily weighted plates to allow the bitter juice to come out. Rinse thoroughly and wipe dry. Beat the egg yolks. Bring the milk to simmering point, pour this into the yolks, stir well, then return to the pan and cook carefully until the mixture is thick. Put aside. Heat the oil, add the aubergine slices and fry until brown on both sides. Lift from the pan, put aside but keep warm. Take out all but a few tablespoonfuls of oil. Fry the onions and garlic until soft. Line the bottom of a 18–20cm (7–8in) pan with a layer of aubergine spread with a layer of meat and one of onions. Repeat this until all the ingredients are finished. Dilute the tomato concentrate with the stock, add pepper, pour this into the dish and when it has penetrated to the bottom, gently pour the egg custard over the top. Put into a preheated moderate oven (180C, 350F, Mark 4) and bake for about an hour until the top has formed a soft but golden crust. Serve hot or cold.

Meat and Potato Pie

MOUSAKA (Greece)

For 6–8

$\frac{1}{2}$kg (about 1lb) minced meat
2 large onions, sliced
chopped parsley to taste
60g (2oz/4 tablespoons US) butter
3–4 tomatoes, peeled and sliced
salt and pepper to taste
1kg ($2\frac{1}{4}$lb) potatoes, peeled and thinly sliced
60g (2oz/$\frac{2}{3}$ cup US) grated cheese
1 cup ($1\frac{1}{4}$ US) béchamel sauce (see page 64)

Put the meat, onions and parsley into a saucepan with a little water and simmer until the water is absorbed and the meat has changed colour. Add the butter and cook gently for 20 minutes, then add the tomatoes, salt and pepper. Continue cooking for 15 minutes. Grease a casserole and arrange a layer of potatoes at the bottom overlapping the slices, then spread with a layer of the meat mixture and continue in this manner until all the ingredients are finished, with the top layer one of potatoes. Mix the cheese into the béchamel sauce, pour this over the top and bake in a preheated moderate oven (180C, 350F, Mark 4) for about 1 hour.

Glazed Carrots

GEZER TSIMMES (Israel)

For 4–6

Carrot *tsimmes* is served at Rosh Hasbanah, the Jewish New Year. Because it is sweet, it expresses a symbolic desire for sweetness all the year round, and, because the Hebrew word for carrot, *merin*, means increased prosperity, the carrot is cut into rings to represent golden coins. The word *tsimmes* means fuss or excitement, and a *tsimmes* can be made with almost any combination of meat, with vegetables and/or fruit, and vegetables without meat. With meat it makes a substantial dish on its own; in its vegetable form it can be used as a side dish.

½kg (about 1lb) carrots
30g (1oz/2 tablespoons US) chicken fat, butter or margarine
1 cup (1¼ US) water
85g (3 oz/½ cup US) brown sugar or honey
15g (½oz/2 tablespoons US) flour
salt to taste

Scrape or thinly peel the carrots and cut them into medium-thick rings. Heat the fat in a shallow pan, add the carrots and simmer until they are a golden brown. Boil the sugar and water together for 5 minutes. Dredge the carrots with flour, stir well, then add the sugar-water, stir well and cook over a low heat until the carrots are very tender. Stir from time to time for the sauce will be thick, add salt and serve hot. This dish can be prepared in advance and reheated.

Rice Stuffing for Vegetables (hot) No 1

ETLI DOLMA (Turkey)

110g (4oz/1 cup US) butter or margarine
2 medium-sized onions, chopped
½kg (about 1lb) lamb, minced
1 cup (1¼ US) long grain rice
2 cups (2½ US) boiling stock
salt and pepper
sage or dill to taste
1 tablespoon (1¼ US) chopped parsley

Heat the butter in a large pan, fry the onions until soft, then add the meat and fry until it changes colour, stirring from time to time. Add the rice and fry this for 5 minutes. Add the boiling stock, seasonings and herbs. Cover the pan with a cloth, clamp on the lid tightly and cook over the lowest possible heat for 15 to 20 minutes, by which time the rice should have absorbed all the liquid. Put aside but keep hot for stuffing vegetables.

Rice Stuffing for Vegetables (cold) No 2

IÇI ZEYTINYAĞLI (Turkey)

1 cup (1¼ US) olive oil (no other oil will do)
4 medium-sized onions, finely chopped
1 cup (1¼ US) long grain rice
½ cup (⅔ US) hot water
1 tablespoon (1¼ US) pine-nuts
1 teaspoon (1¼ US) finely chopped mint
1 tablespoon (1¼ US) currants
1 teaspoon (1¼ US) finely chopped fresh thyme or sage, or about ¼ teaspoon dried
1 teaspoon (1¼ US) finely chopped fennel, or about ¼ teaspoon dried
1 tablespoon (1¼ US) sugar
salt and pepper

Heat the oil and fry the onions until they begin to change colour but remain soft. Add the rice and fry for 10 minutes, stirring frequently. Add the hot water and remaining ingredients. Cover the pan and simmer for a further 20 minutes by which time all the liquid will have been absorbed and the rice cooked. Put aside until cold.

Stuffed Vine Leaves (hot)

YAPRAK DOLMASI ETLI (Turkey)

For 10–12

rice stuffing No 1 (see page 118)
50 vine leaves
juice 1 lemon
1 tablespoon (1¼ US) tomato concentrate

First make the stuffing. Canned vine leaves may be used in this recipe; the usual sized can holds about 50 leaves. The leaves require careful handling. Plunge them gently into cold water, then spread them onto a cloth to dry. Any which are broken should not be discarded but put aside, they also have their use.

Put a teaspoonful of the stuffing on to each leaf, fold in the sides towards the centre over the filling. Now fold the leaf into a neat little roll, roughly 4cm ($1\frac{1}{2}$in.) long, and tie round and round with cotton. It will look like a short, fat sausage. Repeat this until all the leaves and the stuffing are used up. Each package must be securely tied but not too tightly as the rice will still swell just a little.

Line the bottom of a pan with the discarded leaves. If there are none, use either lettuce or cabbage leaves. Arrange a layer of the stuffed leaves (*dolmas*), packing them tightly side by side (like sardines) in order to prevent movement while cooking. Cover with a layer of leaves, then another tightly packed layer of *dolmas*. Continue until all the *dolmas* are in the pan – with three or four layers depending on the size of the pan.

Mix 1 cup ($1\frac{1}{4}$ US) of water with the tomato concentrate and lemon juice and pour this over the *dolmas*, cover with an inverted plate weighted to keep them down, then with the lid. Cook *very* slowly for $1\frac{1}{2}$ to 2 hours. From time to time it may be necessary to replenish the water. Take out the *dolmas*, discard the spare leaves and serve with a yogurt sauce.

Stuffed Vine Leaves (cold)

YALANCI DOLMA (Turkey)

The cooking and preparation of these *dolmas* is the same as for hot. When they are ready, allow the *dolmas* to cool in their liquid without moving the plate. When they are quite cold, but not refrigerator cold (as this ruins their flavour), drain off the liquid from the *dolmas*, take them from the pan and leave to dry. Serve with wedges of lemon, preferably the following day.

Stuffed Cabbage Leaves

LÂHANA DOLMASI (Turkey and Middle East)

For 6

Stuffing cabbage leaves is international, from Scandinavia right down through Iran and onwards, even to China.

rice stuffing No 1 (see page 118) *1 firm head cabbage*

First make the stuffing. Discard any wilted or badly broken leaves of the cabbage, drop the rest into boiling salted water and cook until the leaves will separate easily. Drain well and cool, then cut off a thick slice from the stalk and carefully pull off the leaves. Lay these flat on a table, cut out the thick centre rib, and fold one side of the leaf slightly over the middle. Put a teaspoonful or so of the stuffing onto each leaf and fold up carefully into neat packages, tie with cotton but do not knot as this makes it difficult to remove when serving. Line the bottom of a pan with one or two spare leaves, add a layer of *dolmas*, another of leaves, packing in the *dolmas* tightly. Add water almost to cover (this can be mixed with tomato concentrate and lemon if liked), and cook over a low heat for about 45 minutes.

Serve hot with a thick tomato sauce or with yogurt.

A simple and time-saving method of stuffing, one which a friend of mine uses, is as follows. Prepare the cabbage leaves as above, to the cutting out of the thick rib. Spread a layer of cabbage leaves on the bottom of an oven-to-table casserole, cover this with a layer of stuffing, add a layer of cabbage leaves and continue thus until all the ingredients are finished, the top layer must be of cabbage. Combine some tomato concentrate with water, milk or yogurt and pour this over the top. Add salt and pepper to taste and bake in a preheated, moderate oven (180C, 350F, Mark 4) until tender, 45 to 60 minutes. If the liquid dries out, add a little more. Serve with tomato sauce or chilled yogurt.

In the Middle East usually crushed garlic is added to stuffed cabbage dishes, or dried mint, or chopped fresh dill.

Stuffed Courgettes

KABAK DOLMASI (Turkey)

For 6

rice stuffing No 1 (see page 118)
12 large or 18 small courgettes
30g (1oz/2 tablespoons US) butter
1 cup ($1\frac{1}{4}$ US) boiling water
salt
2 tomatoes, peeled and chopped
1 small bunch dill, finely chopped

First make the stuffing. Wipe the courgettes with a damp cloth, cut off the stems and scoop out the flesh with an apple corer or thin-pointed knife (this can be used in a soup or another vegetable dish). Push into each courgette enough of the stuffing to half-fill, allowing sufficient room for the rice to swell. Arrange the courgettes in a large shallow pan, combine the butter and hot water and pour this over the top of the courgettes, cover the pan and cook for 15 minutes. Sprinkle with salt, add the tomatoes, spreading them over the top of the courgettes and add hot water to almost cover. Cover the pan and cook until the courgettes are tender, about 45 minutes. Sprinkle with dill and serve the courgettes hot in their sauce.

Stuffed Sweet Peppers and Tomatoes

BIBER DOLMASI and DOMATES DOLMASI (Turkey)

For 6

These two *dolmas* are frequently served together, hot or cold.

rice stuffing Nos 1 and 2 (see pages 118, 119)
6 large sweet peppers
6 large firm tomatoes

First make the chosen stuffing, number one for hot, number two for cold. While this is cooking, prepare the vegetables. Neatly slice the tops from the peppers and tomatoes. Put these aside to use as lids. Drop the peppers into boiling salted water for 5 minutes to parboil them, cool and remove the cores and seeds. Scoop out the pulp and seeds of the tomatoes.

By this time the rice stuffing should be ready. Lightly fill the peppers and tomatoes with the stuffing, re-cover with their tops and put them all in a large, rather shallow pan, they must stand upright and close together so that they cannot fall over and spill out their stuffing.

Rub the tomato pulp through a sieve. Mix this with enough water to come half-way up the peppers and tomatoes and cook the *dolmas* slowly on top of the stove between 30 and 40 minutes, or until the peppers and tomatoes are tender, somewhat crumpled but still firm enough to stand upright, and their liquid absorbed.

Serve with yogurt if serving cold; with tomato sauce if hot.

If preferred, the *dolmas* can be baked, covered, in a preheated moderate oven (180C, 350F, Mark 4) for 40 minutes, or until all their liquid is absorbed and they are tender.

Stuffed Aubergines

BEDINJAN MAHSHI (Syria and Lebanon)

For 6

3–4 large aubergines
oil for frying
1 large onion, minced
1–2 cloves garlic, crushed
225g (½lb) lean meat, minced
2 cups (2½ US) soft breadcrumbs
2–3 tablespoons finely chopped parsley
cinnamon, salt and black pepper to taste
2 eggs, well beaten

Peel and slice the aubergines, keeping the slices as uniform as possible. Heat a fair quantity of oil and fry the aubergines until almost cooked but still firm. Lift the slices from the pan and put aside.

Make the stuffing. Take out and put aside 2 or 3 tablespoonfuls of the oil. Add the onion and garlic to the pan and gently fry until the onion is soft. Add the meat, stir well until it is crumbly and cook until brown. Add the remaining ingredients in the order given, stirring after each addition. Arrange a layer of aubergine slices in a greased shallow oven-to-table baking pan. Spread with a layer of stuffing, cover with another layer of aubergine, then with the rest of the stuffing and finally with a top layer of aubergine. Sprinkle with the reserved hot oil and bake in a preheated moderate oven (180C, 350F, Mark 4) for 30 minutes.

Pine kernels can be fried with the stuffing if liked. Serve hot or cold.

The Fainting Imam

PATLICAN IMAM BAYILDI (Turkey)

For 6

There are many stories concerning the origin of this dish. One is that the wife of an Imam who always took trouble with preparing her husband's dishes, especially aubergines, invented a new way in which to cook them. When the fastidious Imam tasted them he fainted, whether with delight, with shock at the quantity of the oil and its cost, or simply because he had indigestion, no one knows.

6 oval aubergines, fairly large
1 cup (1¼ US) olive oil
2–3 onions, chopped
6 cloves garlic
4 large tomatoes, peeled and sliced
salt and pepper
2–3 tablespoons chopped parsley
1½ cups (2 US) stock or water
1 tablespoon (1¼ US) sugar
juice ½ lemon

Thinly slice off both ends of the aubergines and make a deep slit almost from end to end of each. Heat the oil and fry the aubergines for 5 minutes, turning them once or twice. Take from the pan and put aside. In the same oil fry the onions until they are a pale yellow colour. Take these from the pan with a slotted spoon. Crush the garlic and pound with the salt. Combine the onions, pounded garlic, two of the tomatoes, parsley and pepper and stuff this mixture into the slits in the aubergines. Place the aubergines side by side in a baking dish. Cover with the remaining tomatoes, add the stock, sprinkle with sugar and lemon juice, add a little more salt and the remaining oil, cover and bake in a preheated moderate oven (180C, 350F, Mark 4) until the aubergines are soft. Take from the oven but leave until cold before serving.

Meat Stuffed Courgettes

SHEIKH MAHSHI (Jordan)

For 6

8–12 courgettes, according to size
oil for frying
½kg (about 1lb) minced meat
1 small onion, finely chopped
about 1 tablespoon pine-nuts
salt, black and cayenne pepper
1 cup (1¼ US) thick tomato juice

Wash the courgettes and wipe dry. Heat enough oil to fry the courgettes, turning them to lightly brown all over. Leave to cool. Pour off excess oil, leaving only 3 to 4 tablespoons in the pan. Add the meat and onion and fry until brown, crumbling it with a fork, then add the pine-nuts, salt and peppers. Stir well and continue cooking for a few minutes. Cut the courgettes lengthwise, lay at the bottom of a large, shallow casserole and cover with the meat stuffing. Dilute the tomato juice with 1 to 1½ cups of water, pour this over the courgettes and bake in a preheated moderate oven (180C, 350F, Mark 4) for about 30 minutes. Serve with rice.

For a less rich dish, instead of frying the courgettes they can be boiled in salted water until just tender.

Baked Stuffed Potatoes

BATATA MAHSHI (Lebanon)

For 6

NO 1

6 large potatoes of uniform size
oil

Filling
110g (4oz/½ cup US) soft white cheese
chopped chives and parsley to taste
finely chopped cooked tongue to taste
nutmeg, salt and black pepper to taste
1–2 tablespoons melted butter or margarine
½ cup (⅔ US) sour cream or yogurt

Scrub the potatoes, dry and rub liberally with oil. Prick all over with the tines of a fork. Bake in a preheated hot oven (220C, 425F, Mark 7) until soft, about 1 hour. As soon as the potatoes are cool enough to handle, slice off the tops and scoop out the centres, leaving a thickish shell. Mash the scooped-out potato and mix with the remaining ingredients. Stuff this into the potatoes, sprinkle the top with oil and bake in a very hot oven (230C, 450F, Mark 8) until brown, 10 to 15 minutes.

NO 2

12 medium-sized potatoes of uniform size, preferably oval
3 tablespoons (3¾ US) melted butter
filling (see above)
3–4 tablespoons tomato concentrate
salt and pepper
oil

Choose potatoes which are not going to disintegrate easily. Wash them well, peel and hollow-out the centre with an apple corer. Heat the butter, add the potatoes and fry until they brown, turning from time to time. Arrange the potatoes side by side in a large oven casserole.

Make the filling and stuff this into the potatoes. Mix the tomato concentrate with enough water to come half-way up the sides of the potatoes, sprinkle with salt, pepper and oil, and cover with foil. Bake in a preheated moderate oven (180C, 350F, Mark 4) until the potatoes are soft but not mushy and most of the sauce has been absorbed, 45 to 60 minutes, depending on the size and quality of the potatoes.

The hollowed-out centres can be fried, like chips.

Baked Quince Stuffed with Lamb

DOLMEH-E-BEH (Iran)

For 6

2 tablespoons (2½ US) yellow split peas
6 large quinces (see page 19)
60g (2oz/4 tablespoons US) butter or margarine
1 medium-sized onion, finely chopped
½kg (about 1 lb) lean lamb, coarsely minced
salt and pepper
¼–½ teaspoon ground cinnamon
110g (3 oz/½ cup US) sugar
6 tablespoons (½ cup US) vinegar

Cook the split peas in water to cover until nearly tender, about 30 minutes. Wipe the quinces with a damp cloth but do not peel. Thinly slice the top from each and put aside. Scoop out enough pulp from each quince to make a large cavity but keep the shell intact. Heat the butter and fry the onion until soft but not brown; take from the pan, put aside but keep warm. Add the meat to the pan, stir until it becomes crumbly and fry until brown. Add salt, pepper and cinnamon. Strain the split peas, add with the onions to the meat, mixing well. Spoon some of this stuffing into each of the quinces and place them side by side in a large, shallow oven-to-table pan. Replace the tops, add enough water to come up to a depth of 3cm (1in), cover, bring the water gently to the boil, reduce the heat and simmer the quinces until tender. Gentle cooking brings out their aroma and flavour.

When the quinces are almost soft, combine the sugar and vinegar and baste the quinces with this. Continue simmering for a further 15 minutes. Serve the quinces with the sweet-sour liquid in the pan, either as a starter or as a side dish with roast or boiled meats, or with rice.

Savoury Stuffed Apples

TEFFAH BIL-FORNO (Middle East)

For 6

2–3 tablespoons seedless raisins
6 large firm baking apples of uniform size
6 teaspoons ($7\frac{1}{2}$ US) sugar
110g (4oz/$\frac{1}{2}$ cup US) cooked rice
30g (1oz/2 tablespoons US) butter, melted
powdered cinnamon
water

Soak the raisins in warm water until they are plump. Wipe the apples with a damp cloth and cut a medium-thick slice off the top of each. Put these slices aside. Scoop out the centres of the apples with an apple corer making a fairly large hollow without damaging the shell. Arrange the apples in a baking tin and sprinkle a little sugar into each. Drain the raisins, combine with the rice and butter and mix thoroughly. Stuff this mixture into the apples, sprinkle each apple with cinnamon and cover with their tops. Add enough water to the pan to come about half-way up the apples and bake in a preheated moderate oven (180C, 350F, Mark 4) for 45 minutes or until the apples are soft but still firm. Baking time depends on the quality of the apples.

Serve as a main dish or a side dish to roast meat or chicken. The apples may be served hot or cold as a sweet dish, although for this more sugar must be added, some to the stuffing and extra sprinkled over the apples just before baking.

Poultry and Game

'Chickens, ma'am,' said a man selling chickens in a market in this region some time ago, 'is always with us,' and indeed this was always so, especially when we were travelling through Arab countries in search of a meal. It was a poor Arab cook who could not rustle up a dish of chicken at a moment's notice, and in my day killing the chicken under my nose and in no time at all cleaning and plucking it, then presenting its tough result on the table. But there was no doubt that chickens in many parts of the Arab world were pretty scrawny creatures, scratching their way through life only to come to a sad end. Today things have changed and chicken farms have sprung up in some areas like mushrooms, producing almost a super-abundance of chickens and eggs, even though thousands of spring, or young chickens meet an early end on a spit.

Traditional recipes for stuffing poultry in the Middle East would suggest that the birds were always somewhat tasteless, for these stuffings are exotic and endless. For festive occasions the Iranians stuff their poultry with all kinds of fruit and nuts; the Turks smother chickens with a walnut sauce, and there are variations on this dish throughout the region. After lamb, poultry is the festive meat, so it has to taste good, and all these elaborate stuffings produce the answer.

In Israel chicken is the most popular of the flesh foods, and with their abundance of citrus fruits the Israelis have married the citrus to poultry and have produced some interesting and attractive dishes. One stuffing popular in the country is of preserved kumquats or, failing these, simply orange marmalade.

Most of the Middle East is fortunate in the wide variety of game birds, which include, sadly, many small birds like the lark, a favourite in the Lebanon. But there is quail and partridge, plenty of wild duck in the Caspian Sea region; Iraq has sandgrouse, woodcock, snipe, etc., and in the autumn the skies over Greece are often heavy with migrating birds, many of which alas get no further than a roasting spit.

Roast Stuffed Chicken

TAVUK DOLMASI (Turkey)

For 6

2kg (4½lb) roasting chicken, dressed
85g (3oz/6 tablespoons US) butter or margarine
60g (2oz/½ cup US) pine-nuts
60g (2oz/½ cup US) currants
110g (4oz/½ cup US) rice
2 cups (2½ US) boiling water or chicken stock
salt and pepper

Chop the chicken liver. Heat one-third of the butter in a large pan, add the nuts and fry until they change colour. Take from the pan and lightly fry the liver in the same fat. Return the nuts to the pan, add the currants and rice, stir well, add the boiling liquid, salt and pepper to taste, cover and cook over a moderate heat until the rice is tender and all the liquid absorbed. Add the remaining butter and stir well. Leave uncovered, without heat, for 15 minutes until the rice is dry. Stuff this into the chicken, sew up the aperture or fix with skewers and roast in a preheated moderate oven (180C, 350F, Mark 4) for about 1½ hours.

Pot-roasted Chicken

PILIÇ TENCEREDE (Turkey)

For 6

A usual method of cooking poultry and game in Turkey is by pot-roasting, to achieve tenderness, full flavour and succulence.

Fry 3 or 4 sliced onions in a pan in oil or other fat until they are soft but not brown. Add sliced carrot, garlic, sage, 3 or 4 large tomatoes, or the equivalent in tomato concentrate, and stock to come half-way up the side of the bird. Arrange the prepared bird on top, cover the pan tightly and cook over a low heat until the flesh literally falls away from the bone.

Pot-roasted Stuffed Chicken

TABYIT (Iraq)

For 6

2kg (4½lb) chicken, dressed
salt, pepper and mixed spices
340g (¾lb) long grain rice
225g (½lb) tomatoes
about 110g (4oz/½ cup US) fat or oil
1 large onion, chopped

Rub the inside of the chicken with salt, pepper and the spices (which should include ground cinnamon, cardamom and cloves). Leave for several hours or overnight to allow the flavours to impregnate the flesh. The word *tabyit* means 'to stay' and here it means the chicken should be kept a long time in the spices before cooking.

Wash the rice and soak it for 30 minutes. Blanch, peel and chop the tomatoes. Finely chop the chicken giblets (heart, liver and gizzard) and mix with half the tomatoes. Drain off one-third of the rice. Add salt and pepper and pack this mixture into the chicken. Firmly close the apertures. Heat the fat, fry the onion until brown, add the remaining tomatoes, about 1 cup of water, stir well, then add the chicken. Cook until the water has evaporated and the chicken has begun to brown. Turn from time to time to ensure even browning. Add about 2 cups of hot water, bring to the boil and cook fairly quickly until the chicken is tender. Take it from the pan and keep hot in the oven.

Add the rest of the rice to the pan, some more salt and continue cooking until the liquid has evaporated. Return the chicken to the pan and leave over a low heat until the rice is quite dry and even sticks to the pan, becoming hard on the bottom.

Serve the chicken with the rice. Scrape up the crisp part at the bottom, breaking it up to use as a garnish.

Honeyed Chicken

JEDJAD IMER (Israel)

For 6

1 large roasting chicken
salt
juice 1 lemon
85g (3oz/6 tablespoons US) margarine
4–5 tablespoons honey

Rub the chicken with salt and lemon juice. Melt the margarine, add the honey and beat well until thoroughly combined. Brush the chicken inside and out with this mixture. Put into a roasting pan and roast in a preheated moderate oven (180C, 350F, Mark 4) until the bird is tender, basting from time to time with the rest of the honey mixture.

This recipe is interesting because it is claimed the Crusaders brought it to the Holy Land where it is still cooked by both Arabs and Israelis.

Grilled Chickens with Garlic

DUJAJ MASHWI BE ZAYT WA THOUM (Lebanon)

For 4–6

4–6 poussins
salt and pepper
garlic sauce (see page 65)
watercress

Split the chickens down the back. Wipe with a damp cloth and flatten gently with a kitchen mallet. Sprinkle with salt and pepper and rub liberally with garlic sauce. Grill the chickens on both sides for 15 minutes, basting from time to time with more sauce. Make sure there is a pan under the grill to collect the drippings. When the chickens are tender and slightly blistered, arrange them on a platter, pour the drippings over them and serve with more garlic sauce, watercress, or a green salad.

Fruit Stuffed Chicken

KABABE MORG (Iran)

For 4–6

1 teaspoon (1¼ US) saffron or turmeric
6 prunes
12 dried apricots
1 large apple
60g (2oz/4 tablespoons US) butter or other fat
1 large onion, finely chopped
2–3 tablespoons each raisins and currants
salt, pepper and ground cinnamon
tarragon and thyme to taste
2kg (4½lb) roasting chicken, dressed

Both saffron and turmeric are widely used in Iranian meat and fowl recipes. If using saffron, soak it first in a little water. The prunes and apricots may or may not require soaking before using, some varieties do, others not. However, they should be stoned and coarsely chopped. Peel and chop the apple. Heat the butter, add the onion and fry until it begins to soften, then add the prunes, apricots, apple, raisins and currants, stir and cook for about 5 minutes. Take the pan from the heat, add the seasoning, cinnamon, herbs and saffron water, stir well to ensure the stuffing is perfectly mixed, and leave to cool. Push the stuffing into the chicken, close the apertures firmly and roast in a preheated moderate oven (180C, 350F, Mark 4) for about 1½ hours. Serve with rice, preferably *chelo* (see page 54).

Paprika Chicken with Rice

TARNEGOL BE'PAPRIKA IM OREZ (Israel)

For 6–8

2 medium-sized chickens
salt and pepper
60g (2 oz/4 tablespoons US) chicken fat or margarine
2 large onions, finely chopped
1 tablespoon (1¼ US) mild paprika pepper
225g (½lb/1 cup US) long grain rice

Joint the chickens and rub with salt. Heat the fat in a large pan, add the onions and simmer until very soft, take from the pan and put aside. Add the chicken pieces to the pan and fry to a golden brown. Add the paprika pepper, stir well and take care it does not burn. Add water to just cover the chicken pieces. Cover the pan and cook the chicken pieces until tender. Add salt and pepper just before cooking is finished. Take out the chicken pieces and keep hot in the oven. Bring the stock to the boil again, there must be at least 2 cups, add the rice with the onion and cook over a good heat until the rice is tender and all the liquid has been absorbed. Pile the rice on a hot plate and place the chicken pieces on top.

Chicken with Walnut Sauce

KHORESH FESENJAN (Iran)

For 6

2kg (4½lb) chicken
1 each, onion, carrot, tomato and bay leaf
½kg (about 1lb) walnuts, blanched
2 cups (2½ US) pomegranate juice (see page 177)
salt and pepper

Cook the chicken in plenty of water with the onion, carrot, tomato and bay leaf until almost tender. Take it from the pan, cool and cut into pieces. Strain and keep the stock. Put the walnuts once through the finest blade of a mincer, then combine with the pomegranate juice and stock. Test for sourness; for some people the taste of the pomegranate is too sour. If this is so, add sugar to taste. Put this mixture into a pan and cook it gently until it tends to look oily, add the chicken pieces, salt and pepper and continue to cook gently until the chicken is quite tender and the sauce is a deep *café-au-lait* colour. Serve with *chelo* rice (see page 54).

Circassian Chicken

ÇERKES TAVUĞU (Turkey)

For 6

The recipe for this splendid dish is said to have been brought to Turkey by Circassian girls who helped to fill the Sultan's harem.

½kg (about 1lb) shelled walnuts, blanched
2 thick slices white bread, crustless
salt and pepper
2 cups (2½ US) chicken stock
1¼kg (3lb) cold cooked chicken
walnut or almond oil
paprika pepper

Put the walnuts twice through the finest blade of a mincer. Soak the bread in chicken stock, water or milk. Squeeze dry. Mix the walnuts with the bread and put this mixture through the mincer. Add salt and pepper and mince again. Put the walnut mixture into a bowl, add the chicken stock and stir to a thick sauce. Take off the flesh from the chicken, cut into strips and arrange flat on a platter. Pour half the sauce over the top and turn the pieces until they are all coated with the sauce. Cover and put aside until required. Add the remainder of the sauce just before serving, making sure the chicken is completely covered. Mix about 1 tablespoonful of oil with enough paprika pepper to make a red dressing. Pour this over the top of the walnut sauce. Serve cold as a starter.

Stuffed Turkey

HABASH MAHSHI (Lebanon)

For 12–14

5–6kg (11¼–13½lb) turkey
juice 1 lemon
225g (½lb/2 cups US) long grain rice
110g (4oz/1 cup US) butter or other fat
½kg (about 1lb) minced lamb or mutton
2–3 tablespoons pine-nuts
2–3 tablespoons almonds, blanched
2–3 tablespoons pistachio nuts, peeled
salt and pepper
1 teaspoon (1¼ US) ground cinnamon
2 cups (2½ US) thick yogurt
extra fat for browning

There is an old English saying: 'A turkey boiled is a turkey spoiled'. In the Middle East farmyard birds at one time ranged freely and as a result were extremely tough. Boiling was one of the best methods of cooking them.

Wipe the turkey inside and out with a damp cloth and then rub with lemon juice. Put aside while you prepare the stuffing. Soak the rice in warm water for 30 minutes and drain well. Heat the fat, add the lamb and fry until brown, stirring it frequently with a fork. Add the next five ingredients and continue cooking for 2 to 3 minutes longer, then add the rice. Stir this well into the meat mixture and continue cooking for 10 minutes.

Stuff the turkey loosely with this mixture. Sew up the opening with a strong thread. Draw the legs up close to the body and bind them with thread. Put the turkey into a large pan, just cover with warm, salted water and bring to the boil. Skim, cover the pan and cook gently until the turkey is very tender. Take it from the pan, place in a roasting pan, spread with yogurt and fat for browning and bake in a hot oven (220C, 425F, Mark 7) long enough to brown the outside.

To serve: carve in the usual way. Heap the stuffing in the centre of a large, hot platter and garnish with the turkey meat.

Partridges with Celery and Olives

PERTHIKES ME(H) ELIES KE SELINO (Cyprus)

For 2–4

110g (4oz/scant cup US) green olives, stoned
1 head celery
2 partridges, dressed
juice 1 lemon
60g (2oz/$\frac{1}{4}$ cup US) butter or margarine
salt to taste
1 cup (1$\frac{1}{4}$ US) fresh tomato juice

Put the olives into a pan with boiling water and cook for 10 minutes. Drain. Wash the celery and cut the stalks into medium-sized pieces, discarding the leaves – they can be used as a stock flavouring. Rub the partridges with lemon juice. Heat the butter, add the partridges and fry until lightly brown. Add the olives and celery, cook for 10 minutes, then add salt, tomato juice and enough water to just cover the birds. Continue cooking until the birds are tender. Take out the partridges, cut into halves, arrange on a hot plate and pour the olive and celery sauce over them. Serve with rice or mashed potatoes.

Pigeons in a White Wine Sauce

HAMAAN BI NABEED (Middle East)

For 4–8

3–4 tablespoons butter or other fat
4 pigeons
2–3 onions, finely sliced
2 small carrots, sliced into thin rounds
1–2 leeks, thinly sliced
$\frac{1}{2}$ cup ($\frac{2}{3}$ US) white wine
$\frac{1}{2}$ cup ($\frac{2}{3}$ US) warm water
salt and pepper
8 pieces toast

Heat the fat in a wide, shallow pan, add the pigeons and fry them until brown all over. Take the birds from the pan, put aside but keep warm. In the same fat gently fry the onions, carrots and leeks until the onions begin to soften; slowly add the wine and water, and flavour with salt and pepper. Simmer until the vegetables are very soft. Rub through a sieve. Return the pigeons to the pan and pour the vegetable purée over the top. Cover the pan and cook slowly until the pigeons are very tender. Take them from the pan, cut each into two and put into a hot oven for a few minutes to dry out. Serve the pigeons on toast and their sauce in a separate bowl.

Casserole of Hare

LAYOS STIFATHO (Greece)

For 6

1¼kg (3lb) hare
225g (½lb) onions, preferably small
1 cup (1¼ US) tomato juice
2 cloves
4 cups (5 US) warm water
about ¼ cup olive oil
2–4 cloves garlic
currants or seedless raisins to taste
1 bay leaf
salt and pepper
a little sugar

Wash the hare and joint into serving pieces. Peel the onions, if small leave whole, large ones must be quartered. Put the hare and onions, with the remaining ingredients into a casserole, mixing them all well together. Cover tightly and bake in a warm oven (160C, 325F, Mark 3) for several hours, the longer the better, say the Athenians. Give the casserole an occasional shake.

This recipe may be used with rabbit, with veal or stewing steak, and a little wine or wine vinegar is often added.

Stewed Hare

TSIVIA (Cyprus)

For 6

1¼kg (3lb) hare
2 tablespoons (2½ US) olive oil
60g (2oz/4 tablespoons US) butter
1kg (2¼lb) onions, finely sliced
4 cloves garlic, finely chopped
salt and peppercorns
1 cup (1¼ US) vinegar

Joint the hare into serving pieces. Heat the oil and butter together in a large pan, add the onions and garlic and cook gently until the onions are a pale yellow colour. Add the pieces of hare, turn them round and round until well mixed into the onions, and fry until they begin to brown. Add salt, peppercorns, vinegar and enough water to cover. Cover the pan and cook slowly until the hare is tender, with the flesh almost falling off the bones.

Equal parts of tomato juice and water may be used instead of only water; and a rabbit can be cooked in the same manner.

Casserole of Rabbit

TAVŞAN GÜVECI PATLICANLI (Turkey)

For 6

1¼kg (3lb) rabbit
salt and pepper
flour
2 good-sized aubergines
fat or oil for frying
1 large onion, peeled and coarsely chopped
1 tablespoon (1¼ US) tomato concentrate
2 cups (2½ US) stock or water
sprig each parsley and tarragon
2 cloves garlic
1 cup (1¼ US) red wine

Joint the rabbit and leave it in cold, salted water overnight. Next morning drain and dry the pieces and dip in flour. Peel and slice the aubergines, sprinkle with salt and leave between two weighted plates until their bitter juice has been drawn out, then rinse well under running water and pat dry. Heat enough fat to fry the rabbit pieces until evenly browned, take from the pan but keep hot. Add the onion to the pan, fry for a few minutes, then add the aubergine slices. Fry these until a light brown on both sides, return the rabbit to the pan and place on top of the vegetables. Dilute the tomato concentrate with the stock, pour this into the pan, add salt, pepper, herbs and garlic, cover and simmer for about 1½ hours, or until the rabbit is tender. Just before the rabbit is ready for serving, add the wine. Take the rabbit from the pan and arrange on a hot platter and pour the sauce over the top.

Meat

From Greece right through to Iran, excluding Israel, if you talk about meat, the inference is it comes from the sheep or goat – in some places goat and sheep are synonymous, one can be asked 'sheep mutton or goat mutton?'. Indeed, so-called goat mutton is often better than sheep mutton. As far as Israel is concerned, there is more variety in the meats used but, in view of the environmental limitations which set the pattern for traditional Jewish cookery, meat has come to be used sparingly, with the accent on cheaper cuts which can be cooked and served in well-seasoned gravies. A great use of offal is made which reflects, better than any other form of meat cookery in this country, the inventiveness of Israeli housewives.

Generally meat cooking in the Arab countries is the traditional cooking of nomads, and the people as a whole have become past masters at the art of roasting on a spit, be it a whole animal or kebabs. Even today roast lamb or sheep is a speciality of the area, and in Iraq it is considered a festive dish, likened to the whole roast ox of Merrie England. Incidentally, nothing of the animal is wasted, including the ram's testicles of which I am not fond, maybe prejudice but they do not look appetising, but, there we are, they are a delicacy in this part of the world. Nor do I care for a sheep's eye thrust in front of me, honour though it might be.

Still, throughout Greece in the spring and summer the air is perfumed with the delicious odour of lamb roasting on charcoal. In the winter they turn to roast pig, the only country in this region that cooks and eats pork.

When not roasting on spits – ovens were not much in use in these countries until recently – meat is combined with vegetables, lentils, wheat and rice, also it is highly spiced and herb-flavoured, then cooked for hours tightly sealed in heavy pots over a slow heat until the meat literally falls into shreds. When searching for meat recipes for top-of-the-stove cooking, one must also look among the vegetables. One important aspect of cooking with vegetables is worth noting, it is extremely economical on meat. With a good selection of vegetables, or wheat, or rice, two pounds of meat can be made to stretch for six people.

On the whole it must be admitted the meat in this region is not of the highest quality and never has been, which accounts for the numerous dishes calling for minced meats – minced raw, not cooked. Meat too is almost always marinated in olive oil and lemon juice, or in yogurt, flavoured with herbs, and turned into dishes over which to ponder and realise that the people of the Middle East have learned to live with their lower quality meat, and make the best of it, a best which often is very good indeed.

Beef Balls

TAFTA KOFTA (common to Arab countries)

For 4

3 slices stale bread, crustless
about ½ cup grape juice
½kg (about 1lb) beef, minced 3 times
2–3 cloves garlic, crushed
2–3 onions, minced
2–3 tablespoons grated cheese
chopped fresh dill to taste
salt, black and cayenne pepper to taste
2–3 eggs, well beaten
oil or fat for frying

Soak the bread in the grape juice, then squeeze dry, letting the grape juice fall into a small bowl. Combine the meat and bread and knead thoroughly. Add the remaining ingredients (except oil) in the order given, kneading continuously. Wet the palms of the hands with the squeezed-out grape juice and shape the mixture into small balls. Heat the oil to boiling point, add the meat balls and turn once, then lower the heat and continue frying until the balls are brown all over. Serve hot with a sauce.

Steak Mould

MANTALI (common to Arab countries)

For 4–6

675g (1½lb) stewing steak
3–4 tablespoons olive oil
60g (2oz/4 tablespoons US) flour
1 cup (1¼ US) meat stock
salt and pepper
2 large eggs, well beaten
½ cup (⅔ US) double cream
2–3 carrots, diced
110g (¼lb) french beans, chopped
225g (½lb) button mushrooms
30g (1oz/2 tablespoons US) butter or margarine

Wipe the meat with a damp cloth and mince three times. Heat the oil, add the flour, stir well and cook for 5 minutes. Gradually add the stock, stirring all the time until the sauce is thick. Add the meat and seasonings. Take the pan from the stove and stir in the eggs. Return the pan to the heat and simmer for 5 minutes, stirring frequently. Add the cream and pour the mixture into a well-oiled ring mould. Steam for 1½ hours. Towards the end of cooking time, cook the carrots and beans in lightly salted water for 6 to 7 minutes, or until tender. Add the mushrooms, continue cooking for a few minutes, drain and toss in butter.

To serve, turn out the mould on to a hot dish, fill the centre with the cooked vegetables and serve with plain boiled potatoes.

Kibbeh or **Kubbah** or **Kibbe** even **Kibba**

There are various types of *kibbeh*, varying basically only in shape, the mixture always being the same, minced meat and cracked wheat (*burghal*). Both the Lebanon and Syria consider *kibbeh* in whatever form as a national dish. One of the most popular ways of serving it is raw, although perhaps tray *kibbeh* is equally popular. Then there are *kibbeh* which are hollow inside and stuffed with a few pine-nuts. In Iraq they have a boiled version; Syria, especially in Aleppo, makes a speciality of grilling *kibbeh* rissoles on skewers. But *kibbeh* can be roasted over charcoal, baked in the oven, and fried, it is up to the cook. *Kibbeh* is served only on happy occasions, never when a family is in mourning, or at a farewell meal.

The preparation of the meat for *kibbeh* when made traditionally, by endless pounding, is dramatic, perhaps one way of describing the hammering that used to shake our flat when our neighbours were all pounding away with pestle and mortar until their meat became a sticky paste.

However, all this pounding can be avoided in my heretic opinion by using a mincer and, although probably not the same degree of stickiness is obtained, a very acceptable *kibbeh* is arrived at.

Raw Kibbeh

KIBBEH NAYYA (Lebanon)

For 6–8

110g (4oz/scant cup US) cracked wheat
½kg (about 1lb) lean, boneless lamb, cubed
1 large onion, grated
salt and cayenne pepper
ground nutmeg, allspice, black pepper to taste
olive oil

Soak the cracked wheat in cold water to cover for 10 minutes, then squeeze out the moisture in a cloth. Put aside. Put the meat through the finest blade of a mincer; mince the onion, combine with the meat and mince these two ingredients together. Add the wheat, mix well and knead vigorously; put this mixture through the mincer and knead again until it is smooth. Add the seasoning and spices. Divide the mixture into 6 or 8 equal portions. Moisten your hands with cold water and shape the meat into round, fat cakes about 10cm (4in) in diameter and 1½cm (½in) thick. Make a well in the centre of each cake with your thumb; pour a little olive oil in the centre of each. Garnish with thickly sliced onions and serve raw with lettuce.

Tray Kibbeh

KIBBEH BI SSANIEH (Syria)

For 10

kibbeh *mixture as above*
fat for greasing the pan
½ cup (⅔ US) clarified butter or oil

Stuffing
225g (½lb) lamb, minced
salt, pepper and ground cinnamon to taste
2 onions, grated
½ cup (⅔ US) pine-nuts

Make the stuffing. Sprinkle the meat with salt, put into a pan and cook slowly in its own juice. Add the onions, spreading them over the meat and continue cooking until the onions are soft. Add the pine-nuts, pepper and cinnamon. Rub a shallow round baking pan 26cm (10in) with fat and spread half the raw *kibbeh* over this, press it down, then spread with the stuffing and cover it with the rest of the *kibbeh* mixture. Cut through into diamond-shaped pieces and run a knife around the side of the pan. Sprinkle with clarified butter. Bake in a preheated hot oven (220C, 425F, Mark 7) for 45 to 60 minutes or until the top is brown. Serve hot with rice, or cold with a lettuce salad.

Beef Stew

KABAB HALLA (Egypt)

For 4

675g ($1\frac{1}{2}$lb) stewing steak
1 small onion, minced
60g (2oz/4 tablespoons US) butter or other fat
4 cloves garlic, crushed
salt and pepper
ground cinnamon (optional)
warm water or stock
coarsely chopped parsley (optional)

Wipe the meat with a damp cloth and cut into cubes. Put into a pan with the onion (without fat or liquid) and cook for a few minutes until all its moisture has evaporated. Add the fat and cook the meat until brown, turning it frequently. Add the garlic, seasoning and cinnamon, just cover with water or stock and cook until the meat is very tender, adding a little more liquid as required from time to time. Serve the meat in its sauce, sprinkled with parsley. A dish popular in Alexandria.

Lamb and Yogurt Pilau

MANSAFF (Jordan)

For 6

1kg (2¼lb) stewing meat, cubed
1 small onion, quartered
salt to taste
2–3 cups yogurt
1 egg, well beaten
2–3 tablespoons oil
110g (¼lb) mixed pine-nuts and almonds
340g (12oz/3 cups US) long grain rice

Bring the meat to the boil with the onion and 4 cups (5 US) of water, adding salt. Cook over a moderate heat until tender. Take the meat from the pan and retain the stock. Whisk the yogurt, add the egg and, in a large pan, bring gently to the boil, stirring all the time to prevent curdling. Add 2 cups (2½ US) of the meat stock (not the onion) and bring again to the boil. Add the meat, a few pieces at a time, and let it all come again slowly to the boil. Heat a little oil and lightly fry the nuts. Put aside. Boil the rice. For every cup of rice use 2 cups of water. When the rice is tender, spread it out on a hot serving plate, cover with the meat and some of the yogurt sauce, and serve the rest separately. Sprinkle with the nuts and serve.

Lamb with Cumin

KAMMOUNIAT EL-LAHM (Egypt)

For 4

1 teaspoon (1¼ US) cumin
4–5 cloves garlic, crushed
60g (2oz/4 tablespoons US) butter or other fat
675g (1½lb) lamb or mutton
about 2 cups warm water
salt and pepper

Pound the cumin with the garlic. Wipe the meat with a damp cloth and cut into stew-sized pieces. Heat the fat, add the meat and fry until brown, turning it often. Add the cumin-garlic and continue frying for about 5 minutes, stirring gently all the time. Add the water, salt and pepper and cook over a low heat until the meat is very tender.

Serve with rice.

The Turning Kebab

DÖNER KEBAB (Turkey)

This Turkish speciality has been adopted by many neighbouring countries and, although not prepared in the house, for it takes an expert to make them, mention must be made of them in any book on the cooking of this region. To eat *döner kebabs* you go to a small eating house, to call it a restaurant would be pretentious, where you are served *döner kebabs* and nothing much else.

The meat for this dish is taken from the rump of a sheep, cut into pieces as long as possible, the sinews and nerves removed, and the meat pounded until thin. It is then left for 24 hours in a marinade of oil, lemon, milk and sliced onion. When ready for grilling, the meat is taken from the marinade, spread with warmed sheep fat, then wound round and round a large spit until it looks like a monstrous sausage, immensely fat in the middle, tapering off at the ends. This is pressed down and trimmed until smooth and rounded. The loaded spit is then fixed vertically in front of a hot charcoal fire which is arranged in tiers or shelves on three sides, leaving the front open. The spit, a few inches from the fire on the open side, slowly and continuously revolves, hence the name, for *dön* means to turn round. When the top layer of meat is a rich brown, the cook carves off thin slices with a sharp knife – and a flourish – the slices falling into a small tray. After carving, the meat on the spit is again exposed to the heat. This process is continued until finally there is nothing left. *Döner kebab* is considered a snack and is served either with fresh mint or parsley, and a glass or two of *rakı* (see page 183).

In Syria veal is used to make a similar kebab called *Shawmirmah*. The meat is marinated in a vast number of spices, including mastic, cardamon and plenty of garlic.

Lamb Kebabs

ŞIŞ KEBABI (Turkey)

Much of the culinary skill of the Turks goes into the preparation of grilled meats and probably the best known of these is the *şiş kebab*, or pieces of lamb impaled for grilling on a *şiş*, or skewer, hence their name. The skewers are long and flattened, pointed at one end and thick at the other. When the meat is threaded on to the skewers, the thick end prevents the pieces from slipping off, while the flatness hinders the meat from twisting round when over the grill. The average skewer holds six pieces of meat and are some 60cm (2ft) long. Usually not less than eight or ten skewers are prepared at a time. In Turkey and the Mediterranean such kebabs are grilled over charcoal, giving them a flavour and tenderness different from any other type of grilled kebab. Usually, but by no means always, they are served slipped off the skewers.

When making lamb kebabs, young lamb is used and, if possible, cut from the bone. Buy either ½kg/1lb or more of boned leg meat, or a leg of lamb and bone it yourself. Hammer the meat and cut into small cubes. Marinate these in a mixture of olive oil, grated onion and peppercorns; some cooks add lemon juice. The least time for marinating is 2 hours but it is better if left overnight.

Impale the meat on to skewers and grill under or over a good heat. Turn the skewers from time to time so that the meat is browned on all sides. As soon as the skewers come from the heat, sprinkle the meat with salt and pepper and serve with a green salad, soft brown bread, or on a bed of rice.

This is the most simple method of making kebabs; it can be varied by putting a bay leaf between each piece of meat, or a thickish round of onion, a chilli pepper, or a wedge of tomato.

Gardener's Kebab

BAHÇIVAN KEBABI (Turkey)

For 6–8

As its name implies, this dish is made with small pieces of meat with vegetables supplied from the garden.

1kg (2¼lb) lamb or mutton
salt and pepper
60g (2oz/4 tablespoons US) butter, oil or other cooking fat
2–3 large carrots, peeled and thickly sliced into rings
½kg (about 1lb) small onions
2–3 large firm tomatoes, peeled and thickly sliced
1–2 sweet peppers, coarsely chopped, core and seeds discarded
yogurt
finely chopped mint

Wipe the meat with a damp cloth, rub lightly with salt and pepper and cut into stew-sized pieces. Heat the fat in a large pan, add the meat, turning it over and over to brown evenly. Add the carrots, cover with water and cook over a low heat until the meat is half cooked. Add the tomatoes, onions, peppers, salt and pepper and continue cooking until everything is soft and the meat tender. If necessary, add a little more water so that roughly 1 cup (1¼ US) remains in the pan when the 'stew' is finished.

Serve the meat and vegetables together, top each plateful with yogurt and sprinkle with mint. Other vegetables such as aubergine, turnip and parsnip may be added or used as a substitute for those suggested. In other words, whatever the gardener has to offer. However, some watery vegetables must be included otherwise the dish becomes too dry.

Skewered Lamb Kebabs

CHELO KEBABS (Iran)

Chelo kebabs, always served with *chelo* rice (see page 54), are popular throughout Iran, indeed there are restaurants which serve only *chelo kebabs*, and there is a ritual in the manner of serving them. First the waiter brings a plate of sliced raw onion for nibbling, then another with butter, and finally a third with two egg yolks in their half shells. Then comes a plate of fluffy, steaming-hot rice into which you at once mix the raw egg yolks. When these have disappeared, you add the butter and then a local condiment, *sumac* (see page 20). By this time the waiter is back again with his sticks of kebabs and tomatoes, two sticks per person.

Chelo kebabs differ from the usual kebabs inasmuch as the meat, being spiced and marinated, is not cut into cubes but pounded until quite elastic, shaped on to skewers to the length and breadth of the cook's hand, then pinched into six good-sized kebabs per skewer. At the top of each skewer small, round firm tomatoes are impaled which are grilled with the kebabs until their skins are blistered. The kebabs are served on their skewers for the customers to slip off as required.

Also served with *chelo kebabs* is the local flat bread, *nane sanjak*, baked on small hot pebbles, which must be served fresh and hot.

Veal Ragoût

STIFADO (Greece)

For 4–6

1kg (2¼lb) veal
85–110g (3–4oz/6–8 tablespoons US) butter or other mild fat
1kg (2¼lb) small onions, peeled
1 cup (1¼ US) red wine
salt and pepper
garlic to taste, chopped
1–2 bay leaves

Wipe the meat with a damp cloth and cut into stew-sized cubes. Heat the fat in a large pan, add the meat and cook over a moderate heat until browned. Add the onions and brown lightly, add the remaining ingredients, simmer for a few minutes, then add warm water to cover. Stir gently, cover the pan and cook slowly until the meat is tender and the gravy thick.

A popular Greek winter dish which also is made with pork, beef, mutton or lamb.

Meat Stew

MARAG (Iraq)

For 4–6

110g (¼lb/8 tablespoons US) mutton fat or clarified butter
1kg (2¼lb) mutton or lamb, cubed
3–4 onions, coarsely chopped
½kg (about 1lb) tomatoes, peeled and chopped
salt, pepper and ground coriander to taste

Heat the fat, add the meat, stir it well and let it brown, then add the onions and cook until these are soft but not too browned. Add the tomatoes, salt, pepper and coriander, stir and continue to cook very slowly until the meat is tender. Serve with boiled rice.

This is a very dry stew, the only liquid is that provided by the tomatoes, so slow cooking is imperative.

Casserole of Lamb

KUZU GÜVECI (Turkey)

For 6

1kg (2¼lb) shoulder of lamb
2 large onions
4 large potatoes
12 spring onions (optional)
1 sweet pepper
3 large firm tomatoes
garlic to taste (optional)
60g (2oz/4 tablespoons US) butter or other fat
fresh dill
paprika pepper
salt and pepper
2 large bay leaves, chopped

Güveci can be baked either in small earthenware individual pots, or in one large earthenware casserole. In restaurants the smaller casseroles are rather more usual and are brought straight from the oven to the table. In most parts of Turkey this dish is available at all times, not excluding breakfast.

Cut the meat into large cubes, cut each onion into quarters; peel and quarter the potatoes; trim the spring onions; chop the sweet pepper, removing seeds and core; peel and halve the tomatoes; and crush the garlic. Heat the fat in a frying-pan, add all the onions and as they begin to change colour add the pieces of meat and fry these until brown. Stir the mixture well, then divide equally into six casseroles. In each divide and add the remaining vegetables, 2 or 3 tablespoons of water and sprinkle with dill, paprika pepper, salt, pepper and bay leaves. Cover with a lid or foil and bake in a moderate oven (180C, 350F, Mark 4) until the vegetables are soft and the meat absolutely tender.

If using one large casserole, the procedure is the same except all the ingredients go into one pot. A *güveci* also can be cooked on top of the stove. Obviously other vegetables can be used in this stew, green beans and courgettes are frequently added, also aubergine when in season and, instead of water, stock.

Lamb Ragoût

YIOUVETSI (Greece)

For 6

This is the Greek version of the Turkish *kuzu güveci* (see page 156). It is a speciality of many Athenian tavernas and served in individual casseroles which the waiters bring hot from the oven and turn out with a deft movement into one's plate. This recipe, however, is for a family dish, cooked and served in one large casserole.

1kg ($2\frac{1}{4}$lb) leg of lamb, cubed
85g (3oz/6 tablespoons US) cooking fat, melted
2 cups ($2\frac{1}{2}$ US) thick tomato juice
salt and pepper
4 cups (5 US) hot stock or water
$\frac{1}{2}$kg (about 1lb) small macaroni shapes
diced cheese to taste

Put the meat and fat into a fireproof oven casserole, add salt and pepper and put into a moderate oven (180C, 350F, Mark 4) to brown. Turn it from time to time. Add the tomato juice, half the stock and continue baking until the meat is tender. Take the pan from the oven, add the remaining stock and bring the sauce again to the boil, add the macaroni and continue cooking on top of the stove until the macaroni is tender and has absorbed most of the liquid.

Serve the ragoût from the casserole, garnished with diced sharp cheese, in Greece a piquant *kasseri* is usual.

Lamb and Cauliflower Pilau

MÁLOUBEH (Jordan)

For 6

1kg (2¼lb) stewing meat with some bone and fat, cubed
salt and black pepper to taste
1 large cauliflower
2–3 slices lemon
oil for deep frying
2 cups (2½ US) long grain rice

Bring the meat to the boil with 5 cups (6¼ US) of water, add salt and pepper and cook until tender. Cook the cauliflower separately until just tender in water flavoured with lemon. Drain and break into flowerets. Heat the oil and lightly fry these. Add the fried cauliflower to the meat, making sure there is the equivalent of 4 cups (5 US) of liquid in the pan, then add the rice. Cook covered over a good heat for 15 minutes, then simmer for another 10.

To serve, traditionally the pan is turned upside-down and the pilau emptied on to a serving dish. Serve with a green salad and/or pickles.

Pork with Celeriac and Egg and Lemon Sauce

HIRINO ME SELINORIZES (Greece)

For 6–8

Although the origin of many Greco-Turk dishes may be in dispute, this one is not as pork eaters stop at Alexandroupolis (Dodeagach).

1–1¼kg (2¼–3lb) lean pork
60–85g (2–3oz/4–6 tablespoons US) pork fat
2 medium-sized onions, chopped
30g (1oz/¼ cup US) flour
½ cup (⅔ US) red wine
handful parsley, chopped
salt and pepper
½kg (about 1lb) celeriac or celery
egg and lemon sauce (see page 64)

Wipe the meat with a damp cloth and cut into cubes. Heat the fat, add the meat, quickly brown it, then add the onions and, as they begin to change colour, add the flour, stir well until this is blended into the onions, add the wine and parsley. Stir well again, add just enough water to cover, salt and pepper and cook over a low heat for at least 2 hours.

If using celeriac, scrub it well in cold water, peel and cut into cubes or thick slices. Add to the pan at the same time as the wine and parsley. If using celery, trim and wash it, cut into short lengths and add about 45 minutes before the meat is ready.

Prepare the egg and lemon sauce just before serving, stir it well into the meat and its sauce, simmer for 5 minutes, then leave the pan on the side of the stove, without heat, for 5 minutes to allow the flavour of the sauce to penetrate the dish.

Pork In Red Wine

APHELIA (Cyprus)

For 6–8

1–1¼kg (2¼–3lb) loin of pork
1 tablespoon (1¼ US) coriander seeds
salt and pepper
red wine

Wipe the meat with a damp cloth, rub with salt and pepper. Cut into fairly large cubes, put into a casserole, add the coriander and cover with red wine. Cook gently until the meat is very tender, adding water to the pan if required. Serve hot with fried potatoes.

Steak in a Garlic Sauce

SOFRITO (Greece)

Many dishes in this part of the world are labelled *sofrito*, and this particular recipe, of Corfu origin, is useful when dealing with steak of somewhat dubious tenderness. It has no exact quantities, the main point is that the sauce should be thick and garlicky.

Cut some rump steak in fairly large pieces, pound well then make slits all over the surface to prevent shrinkage when cooking. Rub the meat with salt and pepper and coat it with flour. Heat enough fat to fry the meat until brown. Sprinkle with flour and mix it well into the meat and fat. Now add a generous quantity of chopped garlic, a whole head if you like, and, when the garlic begins to change colour, add enough red wine mixed with a little vinegar to make a thick sauce. Add water to cover, bring to the boil, reduce the heat and continue cooking slowly until the meat is really tender and the sauce thick. Serve hot with creamed potatoes.

Meat with Chestnuts

KREAS ME KASTANA (Cyprus)

For 6–8

1¼kg (3lb) veal or beef
1kg (2¼lb) chestnuts
2 onions, finely sliced
60g (2oz/4 tablespoons US) butter or other fat
salt and pepper

Wipe the meat with a damp cloth and cut into stew-size pieces. Cut a slit in the chestnuts and either boil, roast or grill them until they are easily peeled of both outer and inner skins, between 10 and 20 minutes. Heat the butter and fry the onions until they begin to change colour, add the meat, stir into the onions and fry over a moderate heat until the meat begins to brown. Add about 2 cups of water, salt and pepper and cook until the meat is tender. Add the chestnuts and cook until they are soft and the meat very tender indeed.

Liver in a Wine Sauce

SIKOTAKIA ME SALTSA (Rhodes)

For 4

½kg (about 1lb) calves' liver
½ cup (⅔ US) red wine
seasoned flour
olive oil for frying
2–3 onions, thinly sliced
rosemary or oregano

Wash the liver in warm water and slice into thin strips. Marinade in the red wine for at least 1 hour; drain, pat dry and lightly coat in flour. Heat the oil and fry the onions until lightly browned. Add the liver, stir it into the onions and cook for 2 to 3 minutes, add the herbs and the wine marinade. Cook gently until the sauce thickens and the liver is tender. Serve hot with creamed potatoes.

Kidneys are cooked in the same manner.

Persian Meat Loaf

KUFTEH GUSHT (Iran)

For 8–10

1 thick slice white bread, crustless
1kg (2¼lb) minced meat
1–2 onions, grated or finely chopped
spring onions, parsley, and celery leaves all to taste, chopped
salt and pepper
ground cinnamon to taste
3 eggs
2–3 tablespoons tomato concentrate
1–2 tablespoons lemon juice

Soak the bread in water, then squeeze dry. Put the meat and remaining ingredients into a large mixing bowl, add the bread, mix well and knead until the mixture is a homogenous mass. Put into a 22½cm (8½in) × 11cm (4in) greased loaf-shaped pan, smooth the top down with the back of a spoon and bake in a moderate oven (180C, 350F, Mark 4) for about 1 hour. Can be eaten hot or cold.

Iranian Meat Cakes

KOTLETE KUBIDEH (Iran)

For 4–6

½kg (about 1lb) minced beef or veal
1 small onion, grated
1 thick slice white bread, crustless, moistened
pepper, salt, cinnamon and oregano
garlic to taste, crushed
fine breadcrumbs or flour
oil for frying

Put all but the last two ingredients into a bowl, mix well and knead very thoroughly. Make meat cakes, any shape or size you like, for this is a matter of taste. Leave in the refrigerator to 'rest' for about 30 minutes. Coat in breadcrumbs or flour. Heat the oil and fry in hot fat, browning on both sides for about 10 minutes.

The *kotlete* can be eaten hot, served on rice or left until cold and served as a picnic snack.

Grilled Liver

MI'LAAQ MASHWI (Lebanon)

Cut the liver into cubes and thread on to a skewer. Rub with oil. Sprinkle with salt and pepper. Grill under or over a preheated hot grill until brown. According to the Lebanese, serve with anything but yogurt which, they say, is not compatible with liver.

In another version of this recipe, MI'LAAQ MASHWI BI TOUM, the raw liver pieces are spread with garlic, crushed with salt, and sprinkled lightly with olive oil, pepper and dried mint, left for 45 minutes, then grilled or fried, and sprinkled with lemon juice just before serving.

Kidneys with Mushrooms

KALWAT (Iraq)

For 6

½kg (about 1lb) calf's kidney
flour
lemon juice or vinegar
225g (½lb) mushrooms
1 cup (1¼ US) meat stock
60g (2oz/4 tablespoons US) butter or other fat
1 cup (1¼ US) dry sherry or Madeira or red wine

Wash the kidney, remove the fat and skin and cut out the cores. Soak for about 1 hour in water accidulated with lemon juice or vinegar. Drain and put into a pan of salted water, bring to the boil and cook for 4 minutes. Drain, cool, slice and roll in flour. Clean and slice the mushrooms. Heat the butter, add the mushrooms, stir well, then add the kidney. Stir again, add the stock and cook gently for 10 minutes. Add the sherry, bring gently to the boil and serve hot, either with mashed potatoes or with rice.

Sweets

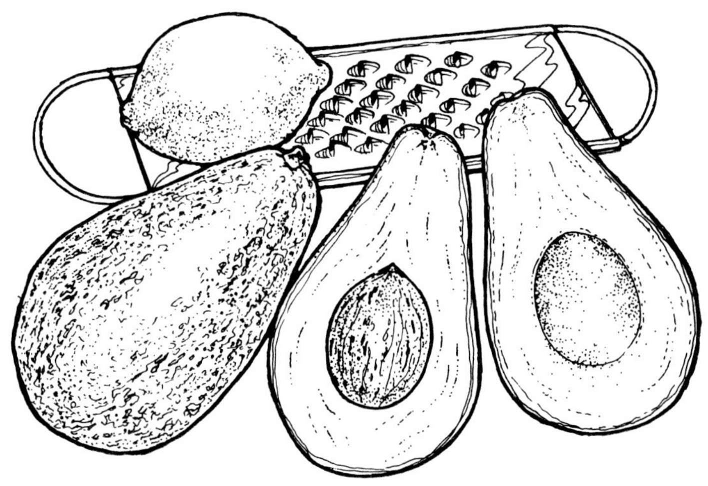

It is said of Mohammed, the Prophet, that he had a sweet tooth, and to him is attributed the saying: 'The love of sweet-meats comes from Faith.' Also, among Moslems, there is the saying:

> The Faithful are sweet,
> The wicked are sour.

Well, the Greeks are not Moslem but their taste for sweets of all kinds would surely win them a place in Paradise, if that is how one gets there. One is tempted to credit the Turks with the origin of all the sweets which appear from Greece through to Iran, but this is probably not the case. Many are simply varied kinds of cakes and pastries saturated in honey or sugar syrups.

Probably the best known of these syrup-soaked pastries is *baklava* (this name is fairly consistent throughout the region), a sort of *mille feuille* which consists of layers of pastry, so thin that as many as 50 layers can be used, stuffed with nuts and soaked in syrup. Another favourite is *kadayif* which also has variations. One called Palace Bread is made with a type of flat bread soaked in honey. Another is a kind of shredded pastry and looks like rounds of Shredded Wheat, and yet another with rounds of crumpet-type pastry, both honey soaked. Then there are the many fritters, similar to the French *beignets* with enchanting names like 'Ladies' Lips', or doughnuts called 'Ladies' Dimples'. In Greece I recollect a pastry so filled with crushed almonds it was almost a marzipan. Athens too, for me, has memories of walnut cakes and a sweet called *melogarida*, which is honey and walnuts pressed together between two wafers to make a hard sticky mass. The Greeks, too, had a *kataifi* which they called *Laïs*, named after a famous courtesan whose love was so sweet. Often these sticky cakes and pastries are served with a kind of unsweetened clotted cream, *kaymak*, which does take off some of the honey-sweetness. This is served only in the cooler months and is so stiff it can be cut with a knife. *Halva* one finds throughout this region, in most parts it is made with a butter, sugar, honey and flour combination, flavoured with rose-water or saffron. In Greece they make *halva* with semolina, producing a solid but extremely pleasant eating cake.

Who produces the most varieties or the best small cakes, or what the Americans so aptly call cookies, is a matter for local pride, not for me to judge. In every town it seems to me that shop after shop is filled with enticing small cakes, all very tempting to the sweet-toothed, all beautifully arranged, all lucious and good to eat. I feel sure though that *lokum* is a

Turkish speciality for we have it on good authority it was invented by a Turk, but one never knows. It is made with a mixture of cornflour and sugar, nuts and rose-water, cooked to a thick, jelly-like consistency, set and then cut into cubes and rolled in powdered sugar.

I think I first met the custom of offering 'spoon sweets' to guests in Greece, but it is done elsewhere, certainly in Iran. This consists of offering guests a tray with glasses of home-made preserves, some glasses filled with water, spoons, small glasses of liqueur or cups of Turkish coffee. The guest is meant to take a spoon and with this pick up a spoonful of the preserve and eat it. With the spoon still in his hand, he drinks a glass of water, returns the glass to the tray and puts his spoon in it. He then accepts a glass of liqueur or a cup of coffee, after which he wishes his hostess and her family happiness and good fortune.

The usual finish to a meal throughout the region is fresh fruit. In the summer months this will be a bowl of iced fruit, in the winter months probably a salad of dried fruits or maybe a compôte. Even the milk puddings, so popular throughout the region, are not designed as a finish to a meal but to be eaten when the mood takes one. However, I find these milk puddings excellent, especially after a rather rich or heavy meal for they are delicate in flavour, light and refreshing.

A note on the puddings of Israel. As with all their cooking, the Israelis seem to have the best of all worlds. Just as they have the cooking of savoury dishes from Jews coming from East and West, so they have puddings ranging from those originating in India to those in the USA.

For the recipes in this chapter, I have chosen the more simple ones. This is not to say that the home cook cannot make the many sugary cakes and pastries so beloved of the region, but nowadays, even the Turkish, Greek and Arab housewives buy their pastries in famous and favourite pastryshops. And with the migration of people, many of these pastries are now familiar in the West, not only in those shops which specialise in unusual foods but in general pastryshops.

Cheesecake

OOGAT G'VNA (Israel)

For 8

Biscuit Pastry

Roll out 18 digestive or similar biscuits and crush into fine crumbs. Mix these with between a quarter or half a cup of melted butter or margarine and about 1 tablespoonful of fine sugar. Press the crumbs firmly on the bottom and round the sides of a loose-bottom or spring-form baking tin 23cm (9in) in diameter.

Filling

- *½kg (about 1lb) curd cheese*
- *1 teaspoon (1¼ US) vanilla essence*
- *2 tablespoons (2½ US) granulated sugar*
- *3 tablespoons (3¾ US) sifted flour*
- *pinch salt*
- *5 egg yolks*
- *1 tablespoon (1¼ US) lemon juice*
- *1 cup (1¼ US) thick cream*
- *5 egg whites*
- *60g (2oz/¼ cup US) castor sugar*

Cream the cheese, add the vanilla and beat well; add the granulated sugar and flour, beating all the time; add salt and continue beating until the mixture is light and fluffy. Add the egg yolks, each one separately, beating vigorously at each addition. Add the lemon juice and cream, still beating. Beat the egg whites until stiff, then add the castor sugar and beat until the mixture is smooth and glossy, like a meringue. Fold the egg whites into the cheese mixture – do this with a light but firm touch. Pour the mixture into the baking pan and bake in a preheated moderate oven (180C, 350F, Mark 4) for 1 hour or until the top is brown. Turn off the heat and let the cheesecake cool in the oven – if taken out immediately, it will flop in the centre.

Easter Cakes

MA'AMOUL (Lebanon)

Makes 35–40 cakes

½kg (about 1lb) fine semolina
1 cup (1¼ US) clarified butter (see page 16)
1 cup (1¼ US) boiling water
1 cup (1¼ US) chopped walnuts
170g (6oz/¾ cup US) sugar
1 teaspoon (1¼ US) orange blossom essence or water
1 teaspoon (1¼ US) rose-water
powdered sugar for dredging

In the Lebanon these traditional little Easter cakes are moulded in the bowls of decoratively carved spoons before being baked.

Put the semolina into a mixing bowl, cut in the butter, mix well then add the boiling water and mix to a dough. Turn out on a lightly floured board and knead well. Cover tightly and leave in a cool place overnight. Next day knead again and break off small lumps and roll into balls the size of a walnut. Hollow-out the centres. Combine the walnut meats, sugar, orange blossom water and rose-water and put a little of this mixture into each cake. Press the dough over the filling. If you have a wooden spoon with a deep, carved bowl, then mould the cakes in this, otherwise simply put the cakes on to a baking sheet, make a pattern on each with the tines of a fork. Bake in a preheated moderate oven (180C, 350F, Mark 4) until lightly browned, 20 to 25 minutes. While still hot, generously dredge with powdered sugar.

Orange Custard with Caramel

BOURTAKA MUHALLABIEH (Lebanon)

For 4–6

4 eggs, lightly beaten
4 tablespoons (5 US) castor sugar
pinch salt
3 cups ($3\frac{3}{4}$ US) milk, scalded
vanilla sugar or essence to taste
4–6 oranges, peeled and thinly sliced
225g ($\frac{1}{2}$lb) granulated sugar
2 tablespoons ($2\frac{1}{2}$ US) hot water

Mix the eggs and castor sugar in the top of a double boiler, add salt and gradually the scalded milk, stirring all the time. Put the pan over boiling water (make sure it does not touch the water, otherwise the sauce will curdle) and, stirring constantly, cook until the custard thickens. Take the pan from the hot water and steep in cold water to cool the custard. Add the vanilla.

Arrange the orange slices in a shallow glass dish. When the custard is cold, beat it well then pour it over the oranges. Heat the granulated sugar in a heavy pan until it is melted but not browned, then slowly add the hot water. Stir well, cook for a minute then pour while hot over the top of the custard.

Cornflour Pudding

CREMA (Cyprus)

For 4

3 tablespoons ($3\frac{3}{4}$ US) cornflour
4 cups (5 US) milk
rose-water
3 tablespoons ($3\frac{3}{4}$ US) castor sugar
hazel-nuts, coarsely ground

Mix the cornflour to a thin paste with some of the milk and 2 tablespoons ($2\frac{1}{2}$ US) of rose-water. Bring the remainder of the milk with the sugar to the boil and gradually add the cornflour paste, stirring all the time. Cook gently, still stirring, for 10 minutes. Rinse a mixing bowl with rose-water, pour the cornflour mixture into this and beat it until it is absolutely smooth. Rinse 4 small bowls with rose-water and pour enough of the cornflour pudding into each to come to the top of the bowl. Sprinkle generously with hazel-nuts and leave to chill in the refrigerator.

Puddings of this kind are eaten between meals throughout the region.

Cold Rice Pudding

SÜTLÂC (Turkey)

For 4–6

4 cups (5 US) milk
¼ cup (⅓ US) water
3 tablespoons (3¾ US) short grain rice
45g (1½oz/½ cup US) ground rice
110g (4oz/½ cup US) sugar
powdered cinnamon

Combine the milk and water and bring to the boil. Add the short grain rice, stirring all the while, and cook for 10 minutes. Take a little of the milk from the pan and mix the ground rice to a smooth paste. Stir this into the rice, add the sugar, again stir well and continue cooking for another 10 minutes, stirring from time to time. Beat thoroughly until the mixture is cool, then pour the rice into small bowls and leave until cold before serving. Sprinkle with powdered cinnamon and serve in the bowls.

Like CREMA (see page 169), served between meals.

Ground Rice Pudding with Rose-water

KAZANDIBI (Turkey)

For 4

85g (3oz/½ cup US) ground rice
2 cups (2½ US) milk
110g (4oz/½ cup US) sugar
2 tablespoons (2½ US) rose-water

Soak the rice in the milk for 15 minutes then cook in the top of a double boiler until thick. Stir continuously. Add the sugar and rose-water, beat the mixture well, take from the heat, continue to beat until the rice is cool, then divide into 4 small bowls and leave until cold. Serve with rose-water.

Noodle Pudding

LOCKSHEN (Israel)

For 6

A festival dairy dish but good at any time.

225g (½lb) fine noodles or vermicelli
1 teaspoon (1¼ US) salt
60g (2oz/4 tablespoons US) margarine
2–3 eggs, well beaten
110g (¼lb/⅔ cup US) seedless raisins or sultanas
60g (2oz/heaped ½ cup US) mixed peel, finely chopped
60g (2oz/4 tablespoons US) sugar
good pinch ground cinnamon
1 cup (1¼ US) orange juice or other fruit juice
margarine for greasing the dish

Cook the noodles in rapidly boiling salted water until just tender. Drain, drop into a mixing bowl, add the margarine, stir well, then add the next six ingredients, mixing gently but thoroughly. Generously grease a shallow baking dish, turn the noodle mixture into this and bake for 30 to 40 minutes in a moderate oven (180C, 350F, Mark 4).

Finely chopped nuts also may be added, and narrow flat noodles used instead of fine.

Semolina Halva

HALVAS SIMIGTHALENIOS (Greece)

For 12

The secret of a good semolina halva is to cook the semolina in butter until it is a golden brown and has a slightly nutty flavour. Use either British or American cups in this recipe.

1½ cups sugar
2 cups water
110g (¼lb/½ cup US) unsalted butter
1 cup coarse semolina

Garnish
almonds, peeled and coarsely chopped
ground cinnamon

Combine the sugar and water in a small pan, cook slowly, stirring all the time until the sugar dissolves, then cook until it forms a syrup. Heat the butter in a thick pan over a low heat to boiling point, add the semolina, stir with a wooden spoon and slowly cook the semolina until it is a golden brown. Add the syrup, stir until it is blended into the semolina, cover the pan with a napkin and leave over the lowest possible heat, or in a warm oven, *not hot*, for 15 minutes. By this time the semolina should have absorbed the syrup. Put it into a lightly greased mould, press it down firmly and leave until quite cold. Turn out to serve, generously garnished with almonds and sprinkled with cinnamon.

Cream in Paradise

YAKH DAR BEHISHT (Iran)

For 4–6

60g (2oz/¼ cup US) sugar
60g (2oz/scant ⅓ cup US) almonds, blanched and chopped
3 eggs, separated
110g (¼lb/½ cup US) unsalted butter
½ cup (⅔ US) double or thick cream

A rich pudding which requires no cooking but, instead, a strong elbow or, better still, a blender.

First make a praline. Melt the sugar, stir until it begins to brown, then add the almonds. Pour the mixture on to a cold slab, leave until it is cold and hard, then break it up and crush to almost a powder. Beat the butter until it is very light and frothy, the original recipe says 'for 30 minutes'. Beat the egg yolks until smooth and thick, the whites until stiff. Gradually add the yolks to the butter, beating all the time until the mixture becomes almost spongey; beat in the cream, the pounded praline, and finally fold in the egg whites. Pour this mixture into a mould and leave until set. Turn out to serve.

A variation of this recipe is to line the mould with Savoy biscuits.

Pumpkin and Walnut Pudding

SHIRINI (Iraq-Kurdish)

For 4

110g (6oz/$\frac{3}{4}$ cup US) sugar
$\frac{1}{2}$ cup ($\frac{2}{3}$ US) water
$\frac{1}{2}$kg (about 1lb) pumpkin
110g ($\frac{1}{4}$lb/1 cup US) walnuts, chopped
thick cream

Cook the sugar and water to a thick syrup. (The sugar must be cooked to a syrup as this caramelizes the pumpkin and it cooks until soft without becoming mushy.) Peel the pumpkin, remove the seeds and chop the flesh into cubes. Cook this in the syrup until it is thick and soft and has absorbed almost all of the syrup. Arrange the pumpkin on a plate and sprinkle it with walnuts. Serve with a thick cream, preferably clotted.

Instead of walnuts, the pumpkin can be sprinkled with lemon juice and shredded coconut.

Avocado Ice-Cream

GLIDAT AVOCADO (Israel)

For 4

2 large ripe avocados
good pinch salt
2 tablespoons ($2\frac{1}{2}$ US) lime or lemon juice
1 teaspoon ($1\frac{1}{4}$ US) grated lime or lemon rind
85g (3oz/$\frac{1}{4}$ cup US) clear mild honey

The honey for this dish should not have too strong an aroma, otherwise it will kill the delicate flavour of the avocado.

Cut the avocados into halves, remove the stones and scoop out the flesh. Combine with the remaining ingredients and mash until smooth, then rub through a fine sieve. Put into a container and freeze for about 4 hours.

Shiraz Date Cake

RANGINAK (Iran)

For 6

½kg (about 1lb) dates
225g (½lb) walnuts, shelled and coarsely crushed
110g (4oz/½ cup US) unsalted butter
110g (4oz/1 cup US) flour
1 tablespoon (1¼ US) cinnamon or to taste
30g (1oz/2 tablespoons US) sugar

Carefully stone the dates and stuff with walnuts. Put into a cake pan (preferably a spring-form), each date standing upright and packed together tightly. Press down firmly. Heat the butter and gradually stir in the flour, simmering until the mixture is a golden brown. Spread this over the dates, level the top down with the back of a spoon, and leave until cold. Mix the cinnamon with the sugar and sprinkle over the cake just before serving.

Makes a cake 15cm (6in) in diameter and 4cm (1½in) thick.

Date Halva

HALAWA TAMR (Iraq)

For 6

450g (1lb) dates, stoned and chopped
450g (1lb) walnuts, shelled and coarsely chopped

Combine these ingredients, knead until smooth, cut into squares and serve with cream.

Stewed Prickly Pears

SABRA MEVUSHAL (Israel)

For 4

This is the fruit of a cactus and its name, *sabra*, has come also to mean affectionately in Israel the native-born Israeli, prickly on the outside but tender inside, qualities which the Israelis feel they share with the cactus pear. *Sabras* are extremely good to eat, but must be handled with gloves when peeling for their prickles are nasty. The flesh, which is a pale greenish-cum-yellow colour, can be eaten raw or gently stewed, as in this recipe. In Israel peeled *sabras* are sold on the street corners when in season and kept on ice. In homes peeled *sabras* are served raw, chilled and sprinkled with lemon juice and powdered sugar.

225g (½lb/1 cup US) sugar
2½ cups (3 US) water
few drops cochineal
16 prickly pears, peeled
juice 1 lemon
powdered sugar

Boil the sugar and water until a thin syrup is formed. Add the cochineal and stir well. Add the pears to the syrup and simmer for exactly 3 minutes. Remove the pan from the heat, add the lemon juice, stir gently then turn the pears with their syrup into a glass dish and leave until cool. Sprinkle with powdered sugar when serving.

In Israel a liqueur called *Sabra* is made from prickly pears.

Pomegranate Juice

ABI ANAR (Iran)

Squeezing the juice from pomegranates is not difficult. Press all over the pomegranate with the fingers, working hard to crush the pips inside thus releasing the juice. When you feel there is plenty of juice, make an incision in the skin with the pointed end of a sharp knife and let the juice flow out. A good pomegranate will give at least one cup of juice. Strain before using.

Pomegranate Jelly

GELEE ANAR (Iran)

Combine pomegranate juice with gelatine according to the makers' instructions. Add sugar, for most pomegranates are somewhat sour, and leave to jell. To serve, turn out and cover with cream. Although this recipe does not suggest it, I add red table wine to the juice.

Drinks and Beverages

Water

Most of the countries included in this book are arid regions where water is at a premium, and naturally treated as a life-giving blessing. This attitude reaches its zenith in Turkey. Water to a Turk is like wine to a Frenchman, and treated with the same respect. A connoisseur, he names it, bottles it and places it on the table with as much reverence he would with a vintage wine. Families will spend their Sundays on excursions to a favourite spring or well and return home laden with bottles of water for, although tap water in towns is equal to water anywhere, the Turks for taste prefer spring water and even buy it from street vendors.

Tea

Tea is drunk throughout the Middle East but reaches its peak in Iran and Iraq. Usually tea is made in a samovar heated by charcoal, the fumes escaping through a vertical flue. When the water boils in the samovar it is poured from a tap over tea leaves in a china pot which is then placed on top of the samovar where the tea stews. Served in narrow-waisted glasses (*istikhans*), the tea is heavily sweetened, a thick layer of sugar filling the lower part of the glass. In some areas, particularly Iran, a lump of sugar is often retained in the mouth while the tea is drunk. Travelling through Iran one is eternally grateful to the *chaikhanas*, tea houses, where scalding glasses of sweet, milkless tea are served which, strangely, are cooling.

Teas or *tisanes* are made from various herbs, brewed for their medicinal properties. In Baghdad they make a refreshing tea with *numi Basrah* (*qv*), and a 'blue' tea from a variety of the blue anchusa flower, offered to those suffering from a fever, while a violet tea, made from a special variety of violet, is considered efficaceous against measles; camomile tea is esteemed for almost all complaints, including sleeplessness.

Coffee

According to legend, coffee was first appreciated at the beginning of the ninth century A.D. by a Mufti of Aden who discovered that it kept the dervishes awake at night during their long prayers. It was introduced into Turkey in the reign of Suleiman the Magnificent (1520–66) by a merchant from Aleppo. The Arabic name for the beverage was *kahveh* which, like wine, was credited with properties which quelled the appetite. Naturally this excited the suspicions of the more devout Moslems who viewed the development of the coffee house with stern disapproval. But Suleiman permitted them and they became general throughout his empire. Thus the cult of the coffee house spread to Iran and the Balkans where today the habit of drinking coffee is as important as in Turkey itself. A great deal of business is conducted over cups of coffee and I am told that in Egypt some businessmen print the name of their favourite coffee house on their visiting cards.

But, no matter where you are in this region, among rich and poor, in towns and remote hamlets, you will always be offered coffee. It is a sign of true hospitality, both in the giving and receiving. For the Arabs, coffee should be taken without sugar or milk, 'as black as night, as bitter as death, and as hot as love'. For the Arabs of the desert, the making of coffee is a ceremonial ritual which begins in the morning when the coffee is ground and, like so much in the culinary life of the Arabs, there is considerable noise made in its preparation, especially in the grinding. But those resounding bangs of the pestle in the mortar are not made merely for fun, they work as an alarm clock, to tell all round that coffee is being made, therefore, time to be up and doing.

However, the town Arab prepares his coffee in much the same manner as the Turk and, as in Turkey, coffee beans are ground in specially designed grinders, long and cylindrical, made from heavy brass (these can be found in many shops in the West). The coffee is ground to a fine powder. For both cooking and serving, the coffee is boiled in a long-lipped brass or copper pot, again not difficult to find. It is not usual to make more than four cups of coffee at a time, usually less. The Arabs drink it from tiny handle-less cups, the Turks from small cups with handles. When the town Arabs do use sugar in their coffee, it becomes almost syrupy sweet.

Arab Coffee

1 part coffee *4 parts* sharbat *or water*

Sharbat is the fluid remains of recently-made coffee. If using water, increase the quantity of coffee. Put the coffee into a small pan, bring slowly to the boil, let it foam several times, lifting the pot up slightly from the heat between each foaming, then leave for a minute or so to let the grounds settle. Arabs often flavour their coffee with a spice, it can be a pod of cardomon, or crushed cloves, a pinch of saffron, and, in Egypt, even ambergris.

Turkish Coffee

For 1 cup

1 coffee cup water
1 heaped teaspoon coffee
sugar (optional)

Put the water into a small pan, bring to the boil, add the coffee carefully so that it rests on the top of the water. If using sugar, let this rest on top of the coffee. Bring the water once to the boil, take from the heat, let the froth die down but do not stir. Return the pot to the stove, let the coffee boil once more, remove from the heat until the foam dies down, and repeat this process twice, then stir the coffee and sugar into the water. Put a little of the froth into the cup, add the coffee and serve hot. The froth brings good luck.

Real Turkish coffee addicts drink their coffee down to its dregs and then spend their time happily chewing the grounds. In both Turkey and Greece a pet diversion is the reading of the coffee cup, the Greeks being very adept at this method of fortune telling. The emptied cup is covered with its saucer very tightly, then the cup is swirled by the drinker to describe three circles with it in the air and then swiftly turns it upside down on the table, where it is allowed to cool and the dregs to settle. The seer then reads from the pattern made by the dregs in the cup what the future holds in store. Usually the interpretation is rosy, sometimes ominous, and, curiously, often quite uncannily accurate.

Soft Drinks

It is not surprising that throughout the Moslem region of the Middle East, where wine and alcoholic drinks are frowned upon, soft drinks have attained a popularity and sophistication not found in the West. Although one does see international brands of soft drinks advertised, it is the more interesting local drinks which are more popular with the people and, if tourists are wise, with them too.

Soft drinks of all kinds are served from early morning until late into the night. You can try fresh drinks of carrot juice, orange, black cherry or tomatoes, all pressed in a modern squeezer while you wait. Further along the region, into Baghdad and Teheran, the cafés display large glass containers filled with all kinds of fruit drinks, some of a curious shade of purple, usually pomegranate juice. These so-called sherbets are much appreciated when the temperature soars. The Iranians like to drink sherbet flavoured with rose-water or orange-flower essence; another particular favourite is *sekangebin*, which is a concoction of vinegar, sugar, lemon juice and water.

But probably the most popular drink of all is that made with yogurt. In Turkey it is called *ayran* and made by mixing one part yogurt with four parts water. It can be sweetened or salt added. In Iran another similar drink is made called *mast*, which is yogurt beaten with soda water and served chilled in tall glasses. Baghdad has a pleasant drink called *shenina* made from buttermilk.

Wines

The Middle East is the home and cradle of wine, though nowadays not grown in quantity or quality and never nurtured with the same respect as in the West. Wine was made in Anatolia in 4000 B.C. from grapes, and 4,000 years before that from berries. From Turkey the art of winemaking spread to Greece and thence westwards. Today of all the countries covered in this book, Greece probably makes and consumes the most. This slump through the centuries can be laid at the door of the Moslem ban on drinking alcohol, now somewhat relaxed but too late to make up for the loss. Today Turkey produces some good quality wine that deserves better treatment than it receives, although some of it is exported for blending purposes to the West. In Greece there is more variety in wine production, including the retsina wines which are not to everyone's taste, although I like them. The Lebanon used to be a fair grower but less so these days. Egypt produced wine centuries ago but today the wine produced in the Nile Delta is mainly for home consumption. Israel's rebirth in wine making was helped by the Rothschild family from France and consequently made a good beginning. In Iran wines are not the subject of ardent discussion and, although not consistent in quality, are pleasant table wines, certainly worthy of something better than the bald numbering most of them are given instead of a name. There does not seem to be much of a market among the Iranians for their wines, so probably the good Omar Khayyam was singing to himself when he sang about that 'jug of wine, and thou'.

Spirits and Liqueurs

Arak is the most common drink throughout the Middle East. Called by the Turks *rakı*, the Greeks *ouzo*, the Egyptians *zibib*, and *arak* in the Middle East, it is distilled from the must of grapes or the coco-palm, with the exception of Iraq which uses dates, making their *arak* much stronger, and a fiery drink when made in some villages. However, whatever its basis, this spirit is always flavoured with aniseed. It can be drunk neat, with a chaser of iced water, or water or ice added when the clear liquid changes into a cloudy milk colour. Iranian vodka is good and mixes well with fresh lime juice. Countries like Turkey and Greece make various liqueurs, mostly from the fruits which are abundant in the region.

Index

Also by Robin Howe

Balkan Cooking
A Cook's Tour
Cooking from the Commonwealth
Cooking from the Heart of Europe
A Dictionary of Gastronomy (with André L. Simon)
Far Eastern Cookery
French Cooking
German Cooking
Italian Cooking
Regional Italian Cookery
Making Your Own Preserves
The Pasta Cook Book
Poultry and Game
Rice Cooking
Russian Cooking
Soups
Sultan's Pleasure (with Pauline Espir)
Traditional Home Cooking